THE MOST POPULAR STORIES

in the

#1 New York Times Bestselling Series

Chicken Soup
for the Soul

by

DAN CLARK

"Dan Clark is a primary contributing author to our Chicken Soup For The Soul series, co-author of Chicken Soup For The College Soul, and author of Little Souls-Best Night Out With Dad. Dan is larger than life, one of the greatest storytellers in the world, and one of our most popular and beloved authors. Dan lives by the Success Principles we propagate, and teaches the 'Secret' through his powerful, unforgettable, inspirational masterpiece stories!"

—Mark Victor Hansen & Jack Canfield,
Co-Creators of the Chicken Soup For The Soul Series

ISBN 13: 978-1-721-62626-7

Table of Contents

Puppies for Sale

A STORE OWNER was tacking a sign above his door that read "Puppies for Sale." Signs like that have a way of attracting small children, and, sure enough, a little boy appeared under the store owner's sign.

"How much are you going to sell the puppies for?" he asked. The store owner replied, "Anywhere from thirty to fifty dollars."

The little boy reached into his pocket and pulled out some change. "I have two dollars and thirty-seven cents," he said. "Can I please look at them?"

The store owner smiled and whistled, and out of the kennel came Lady, who ran down the aisle of his store followed by five tiny balls of fur. One puppy was lagging considerably behind. Immediately, the little boy singled out the lagging, limping puppy and said, "What's wrong with that little dog?"

The store owner explained that the veterinarian had examined the little puppy and had discovered it didn't have a hip socket. It would always limp. It would always be lame. The little boy became excited. "That is the little puppy that I want to buy."

The store owner said, "No, you don't want to buy that little dog. If you really want him, I'll just give him to you."

The little boy got upset. He looked straight into the store owner's eyes, pointed his finger, and said, "I don't want you to just give him to me. That little dog is worth every bit as much as all the other dogs and I'll pay full price. In fact, I'll give you two dollars and thirty-seven cents now and fifty cents a month until I have him paid for."

The store owner countered, "You really don't want to buy this little dog. He is never going to be able to run and jump and play with you like the other puppies."

To this, the little boy reached down and rolled up his pant leg to reveal a badly twisted, crippled left leg supported by a big metal brace. He looked up at the store owner and softly replied, "Well, I don't run so well myself, and this little puppy will need someone who understands."

Puppy Love

THE YOUNG BOY who had been wearing a steel brace on his left leg for the last four months walked through the front door of his home with a newly purchased puppy in his arms. The dog didn't have a hip socket, and it walked with a serious limp. The boy's selection of a physically challenged puppy intrigued his parents. The boy had been down-and-out, but with his new companion at his side, they sensed a newly revitalized spirit of hope and enthusiasm emerging from his soul.

The next day the young boy and his mom went to see a veterinarian to find out how he could best help his little dog. The doctor explained that if he stretched and massaged his puppy's leg every morning and then walked with him at least one mile per day, the muscles around his missing hip would eventually strengthen, and the puppy would have no pain and less of a limp.

Although the dog whimpered and barked out his discomfort, and the boy winced and hassled with his own leg brace, for the next two months, they religiously kept to their massage and walking rehabilitation regimen. By the third month, they were walking three miles every morning before school, and they were both walking without pain.

One Saturday morning as they returned from their workout, a cat leaped out of the bushes and startled the dog. Ripping the leash from the boy's grip, the dog darted into oncoming traffic. With a speeding truck only seconds away, the boy instinctively ran into the street, dove for his dog, and rolled into the gutter. He was too late.

The dog was hit and was bleeding profusely from the mouth. As the boy lay there crying and hugging his dying dog, he noticed that his own leg brace had bent and popped loose. With no time to worry about himself, he sprang to his feet, picked up his dog, cuddled it close to him, and started for home. The dog quietly barked, giving him hope and turning the boy's jog into an all-out sprint.

His mother rushed him and his suffering pup to the pet hospital. As they anxiously waited to see if his dog would survive the surgery, he asked his mother why he could now walk and run.

"You had osteomyelitis, which is a disease of the bone," she said. "It weakened and crippled your leg, which caused you to limp in severe pain. Your brace was for support. It wasn't necessarily a permanent condition if you were willing to fight through the pain and hours of therapy. You responded well to the medication, but you always resisted our encouragement for physical therapy, and your father and I didn't know what to do. The doctors told us you were about to lose your leg.

But then you brought home your special puppy. It was amazing how you looked at each other day after day and seemed to understand each other's needs. Ironically, as you were helping him, you were actually helping yourself to strengthen and grow. You obviously no longer need the support of a brace, and today you discovered it."

Just then the operating room door slowly opened. Out walked the veterinarian with a smile on his face. "Your dog is going to make it," he said. The boy learned that when you lose yourself, you find yourself. It is more blessed to give than to receive.

I Am The Greatest

A FATHER PROMISED his son that if he practiced, all day he'd play baseball with him after work. The father arrived home, and they went into the backyard. "Show me what you can do," the father said. The little boy shuffled his feet, threw the ball up in the air, took a swing, and missed. "Strike one," said the dad.

The son repositioned his feet, threw the ball up again, took a second swing, and missed again. His father said, "Strike two."

More determined than ever, the kid dug in deeper, threw the ball higher, and took a third mighty swing. He missed again, spun completely around, and fell on the ground. His father said, "Strike three, you're out. What do you think about that?"

The youngster stood up, brushed himself off, and said, "Man, am I a good pitcher!"

Broken Doll

A YOUNG GIRL was leaving for school, and her mother reminded her to come straight home when her last class ended. Thirty minutes late, she finally walked through the front door. Her mother scolded her. "Where have you been?" she asked. "I've been worried sick."

With a concerned face the daughter sweetly replied, "I walked home with my friend, Sally, and she dropped her doll and it broke all to pieces. It was just awful!"

Her mother inquired, "So you were late because you stayed to help her pick up the pieces of the doll and put it back together again?"

"Oh no, Mommy," she explained. "I didn't know how to fix the doll. I just stayed to help her cry!"

What Goes Around Comes Around

A UNIQUE DIRECTIVE was initiated at a high school in northern Utah, where students with a physical or mental challenge were fully integrated into the mainstream classes and curriculum. To make it work, the administration organized a mentor program that teamed up one special-needs student with a mainstream student who would help him or her along.

The athletic director presented the idea to the captain of the football team. John was a tall, strong, intense young man—not the patient, caring type needed for this kind of program. He made it clear that this "wasn't his thing" and he didn't have time to be a mentor. But the athletic director knew it would be good for him and insisted that John volunteer.

John was matched up with Randy—a young man with Down syndrome. Reluctant and irritated at first, John literally tried to "lose" Randy, but soon John welcomed the constant company. Randy not only attended every one of John's classes and ate with him at lunchtime, he also went to football practice. After a few days, John asked the coach to make Randy the official manager responsible for the balls, tape, and water bottles.

At the end of the football season, the team won the state championship, and John was awarded with a gold medal as the Most Valuable Player in the state. Randy was presented with a school letterman jacket. The team cheered as Randy put it on. It was the coolest thing that had ever happened to him; from that day forward, Randy never took it off. He slept in his jacket and wore it throughout each weekend.

Basketball season started, and John was also the captain and star of that team. At John's request, Randy was again named the manager. During the basketball season, they were still inseparable. Not only did John take Randy to special occasions—like dances as a joint escort for his girlfriend—but he also took Randy to the library to tutor him in his classes. As he tutored Randy, John became a much better student and made the honor roll for the first time in more than a year. The mentor program was unveiling itself as the most rewarding year of John's life.

Then tragedy struck in the middle of the state basketball tournament. Randy caught a virus and suddenly died of pneumonia. The funeral was held the day before the final championship game. John was asked to be one of the speakers. In his talk, John shared his thoughts about his deep, abiding friendship and respect for Randy. He told how Randy had been the one who had taught him about real courage, self-esteem, unconditional love, and the importance of giving 100 percent in everything he did.

John dedicated the upcoming state finals game to Randy and concluded his remarks by stating that he was honored to have received the MVP award in football and the Leadership Plaque for being the captain of the basketball team. "But," John added, "the real leader of both the football and basketball teams was Randy, for he accomplished more with what he had than anyone I've ever met. Randy inspired all who knew him."

John walked from behind the podium, took off the irreplaceable, twenty-four carat gold state football MVP medallion that hung around his neck, leaned into the open casket, and placed it on Randy's chest. He placed his captain's plaque next to it.

Randy was buried in his letterman jacket, surrounded by John's cherished awards, as well as pictures and letters left by others who admired him. But this is not the end. The next day, John's team won the championship and presented the game ball to Randy's family. John went to college on a full athletic scholarship and graduated with a master's degree in education. Today John is a special education teacher and volunteers ten hours a week for the Special Olympics.

The Circus

WHEN I WAS a young boy, my father and I were standing in line to buy tickets for the circus. Finally, there was only one family between us and the ticket counter. This family made a big impression on me. There were eight children, all probably under the age of twelve. You could tell they didn't have a lot of money. Their clothes were not expensive, but they were clean.

The children were well behaved, all of them standing in line, two-by-two behind their parents, holding hands. They were excitedly jabbering about the clowns, elephants, and other acts they would see that night. We could tell they had never been to the circus before. It promised to be a highlight of their young lives.

The father and mother were at the head of the pack, standing proud as could be. The mother was holding her husband's hand, looking up at him as if to say, "You're my knight in shining armor." He was smiling and basking in pride, looking at her as if to reply, "You got that right."

The ticket lady asked the father how many tickets he wanted. He proudly responded, "Please let me buy eight children's tickets and two adult tickets so I can take my family to the circus." The ticket lady quoted the price.

The man's wife let go of his hand. Her head dropped. The man's lip began to quiver. The father leaned a little closer and asked, "How much did you say?" The ticket lady again quoted the price.

The man didn't have enough money. How was he supposed to turn and tell his eight kids that he didn't have enough money to take them to the circus? Seeing what was going on, my dad put his hand into his pocket, pulled out a twenty- dollar bill, and dropped it on the ground. (We were not wealthy in any sense of the word!)

My father reached down, picked up the bill, tapped the man on the shoulder, and said, "Excuse me, sir, this fell out of your pocket." The man knew what was going on. He wasn't begging for a handout, but certainly appreciated the help in a desperate, heartbreaking, embarrassing situation.

He looked straight into my dad's eyes, took my dad's hand in both of his, squeezed tightly onto the twenty-dollar bill, and with his lip quivering and a tear streaming down his cheek, he replied, "Thank you, thank you, sir. This really means a lot to me and my family."

My father and I went back to our car and drove home. We didn't go to the circus that night, but we didn't go without.

One Moment in Time

ONE DAY, HENRY Winkler, the actor best known for his portrayal of Fonzy on the television series Happy Days, decided to take some time off and treat himself to a matinee movie. To avoid fans making a fuss over him, Winkler entered the theater from the side exit door. He shuffled his way into an aisle and found himself a vacant seat.

As Henry turned around to sit down, the little girl sitting in the row behind him smiled broadly, pointed her finger, and slowly said, "Fonzy!" Winkler immediately snapped into the Fonzy character, flipping his hair, swiveling his hips, and glancing left and right. In his signature pose he then pointed his finger at the girl and said, "Whoa!"

To everyone's surprise, the lady sitting next to the little girl passed out. The theater manager went out to assist the woman. Lying in the aisle with a cold pack on her forehead, the woman was asked one question: "Why did you pass out?"

Pointing to the little girl, she replied, "My daughter is autistic, and that is the very first word she has ever spoken in her entire life!"

Rescue at Sea

MY GRANDFATHER SPENT a lot of time in the Netherlands where he witnessed a legendary tale. In a small fishing village in Holland, a young boy taught the world about the rewards of unselfish service. Because the entire village revolved around the fishing industry, a volunteer rescue team was needed in cases of emergency.

One night the winds raged, the clouds burst, and a gale-force storm capsized a fishing boat at sea. Stranded and in trouble, the crew sent out the SOS. The captain of the rescue rowboat team sounded the alarm, and the villagers assembled in the town square overlooking the bay. While the team launched their rowboat and fought their way through the wild waves, the villagers waited restlessly on the beach, holding lanterns to light the way back.

An hour later, the rescue boat reappeared through the fog, and the cheering villagers ran to greet them. Falling exhausted on the sand, the volunteers reported that the rescue boat could not hold anymore passengers, and they had to leave one man behind. Even one more passenger would have surely capsized the rescue boat, and all would have been lost.

Frantically, the captain called for another volunteer team to go after the lone survivor. Sixteen-year-old

Hans stepped forward. His mother grabbed his arm, pleading, "Please don't go. Your father died in a shipwreck ten years ago, and your older brother, Peter, has been lost at sea for three weeks. Hans, you are all I have left."

Hans replied, "Mother, I have to go. What if everyone said, 'I can't go, let someone else do it'? Mother, this time I have to do my duty. When the call for service comes, we all need to take our turn and do our part." Hans kissed his mother, joined the team, and disappeared into the night.

Another hour passed, which seemed to Hans's mother like an eternity. Finally, the rescue boat darted through the fog. Hans was standing up in the bow. Cupping his hands, the captain called, "Did you find the lost man?"

Barely able to contain himself, Hans excitedly yelled back, "Yes, we found him. And tell my mother it's my older brother, Peter!"

Stride to Be Better

I WAS IN Maui, Hawaii, on vacation when Naomi Rhode, a professional speaker, taught me about high expectations. She and her husband, Jim, had been walking along the beach for several hundred yards when she paused to look back to see how far they had gone. She noticed their footprints in the sand and was immediately filled with pride. She pointed them out to her husband and commented, "Wow, think about how many times we have left our footprints in the lives of others."

Suddenly the ocean interrupted by sweeping in and washing away their footprints, leaving no sign of their presence. Naomi was puzzled and almost hurt. She asked her husband, "How can we leave a more lasting impression on people that will not be washed away with time?"

He wisely replied, "Just walk on higher ground."

Rose

THE FIRST DAY of school, our professor introduced himself to our chemistry class and challenged us to get to know someone we did not know. I stood up to look around when a gentle hand touched my shoulder. I turned around to find a wrinkled older lady with a giant smile that lit up her entire face like a Christmas tree. She said, "Hi, handsome, my name is Rose. I am eighty-seven years old. Do you want to get lucky?"

I laughed and enthusiastically replied, "You gorgeous babe, of course I do! Why are you in college at your young, innocent age?"

She kidded, "I'm here looking for a rich husband, you know, get married, have a couple of children, then retire and travel." Hysterically laughing, I begged her to be serious. Her answer was simple but profound. "I always dreamed of having a college degree and so I'm getting one!"

After class, we walked to the student union building and shared a chocolate milkshake. It was obvious we were soul mates, and we became instant friends. In fact, every day for the next three months, we left class together, walked to the union building, and for at least an hour, I sat there in total awe listening to this "time machine" share her life experiences with me. Clearly, wisdom is the gift of the elderly. When an old woman dies an entire library burns to the ground!

Over the course of the school year, Rose became a campus icon and generated attention everywhere she went. She loved to dress up and even occasionally wore miniskirts and high heels! In the third week of school, she even got a tiny tattoo on her left shoulder. I teased her that I was hurt it didn't say "Dan My Man." Of course, it was a magnificent rose.

Every day around 12 o'clock noon, Rose would pause in the library plaza to take a break from walking and attending classes. Within moments a crowd of 50 to 100 students would gather around her to hear and feel the wisdom of Rose. I will never forget the day she taught us that we don't see things as they are – we see things as we are, when she lovingly and tactfully inter-acted with one of our coed friends who had lost her hair in her battle with leukemia. Rose complimented Melody in front of all of us by acknowledging that she never complains and then asked her if there was a dif-ference between dying of cancer and living with cancer, and what was it going to be for her? Whoa! I don't think anyone ever complained about having a 'bad hair day' or took life for granted again!

Rose was so inspirational that I invited her to speak at our end of the season football banquet, and I'll never forget what she said. When I introduced her and she stepped to the podium, she inadvertently dropped her speech and her 3 × 5 cards hit the floor. Frustrated and a bit embarrassed, she leaned into the microphone and simply said, "I'm sorry I'm so jittery. I gave up beer for Lent and this whiskey is killing me! I'll never get my speech back together, so let me just tell you what I know."

As we laughed, she cleared her throat and began, "There are only four secrets to staying young, being authentically happy, and achieving lasting success. It doesn't matter if you're a football player, a professor, a business professional, or an old lady like me. We all need to:

"(1) Carpe diem with humor. Seize each day with laughter. For example, my best friend started walking five miles a day when she was sixty years old. She's ninety- seven now, and we don't know where she is! Ha! On a personal note, my late husband and I enjoyed seventeen great years of marriage. Seventeen out of fifty-five ain't bad! Every night I said the same prayer: 'Dear Lord, I pray for wisdom to understand my man, love to forgive him, and patience to handle his moods. Because Lord, if I pray for strength, I will beat him to death!' Haha!"

"(2) As I've walked around this college campus this year I noticed how many of you football players were still wearing your old high school athletic letter jackets. I wanted to stop every one of you and say, "I know you used to be a stud muffin hunk of burnin love, but when your horse dies, dismount! Stop living in your past. Get a new horsey. Getty up young man. Remember the ten two letter words: If it is to be it is up to me. And remember that the only person you need to be better than is the person you were yesterday!"

"(3) Treat everybody you meet with dignity and respect and make them better because they met you. The same God who made me, made you too!"

"(4) Leave no regrets. There is a giant difference between growing older and growing up. If you are nineteen years old and lie in bed for one full year, and don't do one productive thing, you will turn twenty years old. If I am eighty-seven years old and stay in bed for a year, I will turn eighty-eight. Whoop-de-do! Anybody can grow older. That doesn't take any talent or ability. The idea is to grow up. The elderly usually don't have regrets for what we did, but rather for things we did not do. The only people who fear death are those with regrets."

At year's end, Rose's life-long dream of graduating from college had become a reality. As she walked across the stage to receive her diploma the arena erupted into an epic standing ovation. Unbeknownst to anyone, Rose had been battling cancer for some time, and one week after graduation, Rose died peacefully in her sleep. More than two thousand college students attended her funeral in tribute to the wonder woman who never did anything famous and never made a lot of money. Through her example, she simply taught us that it's never too late to be all you can possibly be!

Support

JOHN MCMASTER BECAME a superstar basketball player in high school. For each of his three years on the team, he was All-Conference, and All-State. In his final season, he was named the Most Valuable Player in the league. John's mother never missed a game at home or away, regardless of the travel distance or weather conditions. She always bought a season pass and was always in the bleachers cheering her son to victory.

Interestingly, John's mother was totally blind. What's the message? Although the mother could not see her son, he could see her. Support makes the special difference!

The Bellman

MY DAD BATTLED cancer for six and a half years. He had a rare cancer called carcinoid that affected his intestines, stomach, and liver. As the pain mounted and Dad's last day approached, I decided I wanted to be by his bedside when he took his last breath. But that didn't happen. I was in Seattle, Washington, on two speaking engagements: a meeting on Friday morning and a convention on Saturday. I was staying at the Seattle Airport Marriott Hotel. It was early Friday morning, October 12. I had shaved and showered and put on my coat and tie when the phone rang. Thinking it was my ride to the convention, I picked up the phone and almost flippantly said, "I'll be right there." But instead, I just stood there.

Fifteen seconds of silence later, my younger brother's voice pierced the quietness of the call. "Danny?" Shocked, I tentatively answered, "Paul? What's up?"

Another fifteen seconds of silence started my heart pounding out of my chest. Then Paul confirmed my greatest fear. "Dad passed away this morning at seven." I sat down on the bed, and the tears immediately started to flow. I asked, "How is Mom?"

He said, "Good."

I said, "Give her a big hug and a kiss for me and tell her I'll phone her in a little while." Paul then asked me what I was going to do. After a moment of consideration I said, "I'm going to go make my speech. That's what Dad would want me to do. He always taught us to only make commitments that we can keep and to always keep those commitments."

I thought it through out loud as I continued to talk to Paul, "I can't imagine what it would be like to be the meeting planner with more than twenty-five hundred people sitting in the audience, and not have the speaker show up. Dad always taught us to keep our promises. I need to stay here and speak and spend the night, speak tomorrow, and then hustle home.

God knows I need your support, and hopefully I can give you some of mine. I know you and the rest of our family and Mom's huge circle of friends will comfort Mom and each other. Mom will understand that my decision is exactly what Dad would want me to do. I'll talk to Mom later today and will see you tomorrow."

I hung up the phone and broke down, crying like a baby. My dad, my hero, was gone! And I was ripped and wrenched with the pain of regrets. Every thought and word was, "I wish, I shoulda, I woulda, I coulda, if only I had." For the record, I've done a lot of pretty cool things in my life (carried the Olympic Torch, flown in fighter jets, won a race-car driving school championship at Nürburgring in Germany, raced dogsleds, and slept in an igloo by the Arctic Sea). But I would trade it all for one more day with my dad! I miss him so much and have too many regrets!

As an author, I love to interview people—especially elderly people (elderly meaning someone older than me!). When I interview someone much older than me, the elderly person will always tell me they do not have regrets for things they did do; they only have regrets for things they did not do. Do you have regrets?

Will you? I did. I still have regrets, and it's a living hell. Religion teaches that hell comes to the unbeliever after death. Yes, true. But I also believe that hell is where the man I am comes face-to-face with the man I could have been! I still have regrets with my dad, and I don't wish regrets on anyone.

Fifteen minutes had gone by when the phone rang again. This time it was my ride, and I told him I would be right down. I went into the washroom, splashed some water on my face to freshen up, left my room, and entered the elevator. As the elevator doors began to close, the corner of a bellman's cart crammed its way through the narrow opening, and the doors "binged" back open. Onto the elevator came an overzealous, way too cheery bellman. He pushed his cart to the middle, forcing me back to the rear corner. Trying to avoid eye contact, I stood with my head down, hands clasped in the "elevator position."

As the doors closed, he blurted, "Yeehaw, Whoa-o-o! Did you see the beautiful sunshine today? I've lived here in Seattle all of my eighteen years, and it's rained every single day. You must have brought the good weather with you. How ya doin'?"

Not looking up, I said, "Fine." He kept staring at me until he again blurted, "No, sir, you're not fine. Your eyes are red and a little puffy. You've been crying."

Instinctively I replied, "Yeah. I just found out my dad died this morning and I'm really sad." The bellman said, "Whoa," and went hauntingly quiet until the doors opened at the lobby. He went left, and I went right to the man waiting to give me a ride downtown to my meeting.

Fast-forward to the introduction of my speech. I had to dig deeper than I had ever dug in my life to rise to the occasion, but I did, and I made my speech. I know it's never appropriate to make yourself the hero of your own story, and I don't mean to. Making my dad proud of me for keeping my commitments and doing the right thing through service above self is the central point of this story.

At the end of my speech, I told the audience I would conclude with a song from one of my albums. I told them the reason I was singing it was that it was my dad's favorite song of all I had ever written, that he had died that morning, and therefore, it would be the first time he had ever heard me sing it in public. I finished the song and speech and had the driver take me to the Seattle Aquarium. Why the aquarium? To run from change? To avoid pain? Absolutely not!

Rather, to embrace every thought and emotion and realize four things: (1) In order to get a better answer, you must first ask a better question; (2) In life there are no mistakes, only lessons; (3) To go higher, you must first go deeper; and (4) Pain is a signal to grow, not to suffer. And once we learn the lesson the pain is teaching us, the pain goes away. That night at the aquarium, I "internally excavated" my innermost beliefs and feelings and remembered we're all going to die, so we have to deal with it by living every day to leave no regrets. Having learned the lessons, I had the driver take me back to the hotel.

I walked into the hotel room, and there on the chest of drawers was a basket of fruit. It wasn't your basic basket delivered from the hotel gift shop with the colored cellophane cover, ribbon bow, and small, sterile, stamped card from the manager that seldom gets your name right—"Thanks for staying with us, Ralphie."

This basket was a broken basket, slightly smashed on one side. It appeared as if it was a last-minute gesture with no resources available. Whoever delivered it was obviously into presentation because the crinkled portion of the basket was turned toward the wall and covered by a big silky rubberized leaf that had apparently been picked off the fake tree in the lobby.

In the basket were two oranges and an apple that had a little bite out of it. (Yes! No exaggeration!) Now, I don't think the deliverer got hungry on the way up to the room and snacked a bit. I believe he was into presentation and had found this huge, luscious, polished red apple that was perfect for his presentation. He couldn't help it if it had a crunch taken from it because the good definitely outweighed the bad and the color was important. The fruit basket also had in it a big ripe tomato and a long, thick carrot. Most important, in my basket was a handwritten note with several misspelled words that said,

"Mr. Clark, I'm sure sorry your dad died. I was off work today at 5:00 pm, but I came back tonight so I could be here for you. Room service closes at 10:00 pm, but the kitchen has decided to stay open all night long so they can be here just for you. If you need anything, just call and ask for me. Signed, James—the bellman."

James was not the only one to sign the card. Every single employee that night at the Seattle Airport Marriott Hotel signed my little card.

Let's put this experience into perspective and briefly rekindle the lesson learned. Here we have James, an eighteen-year-old young man, the youngest person on the entire employee payroll, who "gets it." Here we have James, the lowest paid person on the entire employee payroll, who "gets it." "Gets" what? Service above self; internal stretch and change; behavior that exceeds external expectations; being more than we've been simply because we want to—motivated by the simple fact that we can!

The Art Collection

A FATHER AND son were very close and enjoyed adding valuable art pieces to their collection. Priceless works by Picasso, Van Gogh, Monet, and many other artists adorned the walls of the family estate. The son's trained eye and sharp business mind caused his widowed father to beam with pride as they dealt with art collectors around the world.

As winter approached, war engulfed the nation, and the young man left to serve his country. After only a few short weeks, his father received a telegram. His beloved son had died while rushing a fellow soldier to a medic. Distraught and lonely, the old man faced the future with anguish and sadness.

One morning, a knock on the door awakened the depressed old man. As he walked to the door, the masterpieces on the walls only reminded him that his son was not coming home. As he opened the door, he was greeted by a soldier with a large package in his hand.

The soldier introduced himself to the man by saying, "I was a friend of your son. I was the one he was rescuing when he died. May I come in for a few moments? I have something to show you." As the two began to talk, the soldier told of how the man's son had told everyone of both his and his father's love of fine art. "I'm an artist," said the soldier, "and I want to give you this."

As the old man unwrapped the package, the paper gave way to reveal a portrait of the man's son. Though the world would never consider it the work of a genius, the painting featured the young man's face in striking detail. Overcome with emotion, the man thanked the soldier, promising to hang the picture above the fireplace.

A few hours later, after the soldier had departed, the old man set about his task. True to his word, the painting went above the fireplace, pushing aside thousands of dollars' worth of paintings. As other stories of his son rescuing dozens of wounded soldiers continued to reach him, fatherly pride and satisfaction began to ease the grief. The painting of his son became his most prized possession, far eclipsing any interest in the pieces for which museums around the world clamored. He told his neighbors it was the greatest gift he had ever received.

The following spring, the old man became ill and passed away. The art world waited in anticipation for his paintings to be sold at an auction. The appointed day soon arrived, and art collectors from around the world gathered to bid on some of the world's most spectacular paintings. Dreams would be fulfilled this day; greatness would be achieved as many would claim, "I now have the greatest collection."

The auction began with a painting that was not on any museum's list. It was the painting of the man's son.

The auctioneer asked for an opening bid. The room was silent. "Who will open the bidding with one hundred dollars?" he asked. Minutes passed. No one spoke. From the back of the room came, "Who cares about that painting? It's just a picture of his son. Let's forget it and go on to the good stuff."

More voices echoed in agreement. "No, we have to sell this one first," replied the auctioneer. "Now, who will take the son?" Finally, a friend of the old man spoke. "Will you take ten dollars for the painting? That's all I have. I knew the boy, so I'd like to have it."

"I have ten dollars. Will anyone go higher?" called the auctioneer. After more silence, the auctioneer said, "Going once, going twice. Gone."

The gavel fell. Cheers filled the room and someone exclaimed, "Now we can get on with it and start bidding on these treasures!"

The auctioneer looked at the audience and announced the auction was over. Stunned disbelief quieted the room. Someone spoke up and asked, "What do you mean it's over? We didn't come here for a picture of some old guy's son. What about all of these paintings? There are millions of dollars' worth of art here!"

The auctioneer replied, "It's very simple. According to the will of the father, whoever takes the son gets it all."

A Brother's Song

LIKE ANY GOOD mother, when Karen found out that another baby was on the way, she did what she could to help her three-year-old son, Michael, prepare for a new sibling. They found out that the new baby was going to be a girl, and day after day, night after night, Michael sang to his little sister in Mommy's tummy.

He was building a bond of love with his little sister before he even met her. The pregnancy progressed normally for Karen and in time, the labor pains came. But serious complications arose during delivery and Karen found herself in hours of labor. Finally, after a long struggle, Michael's little sister was born. She was in very serious condition.

The ambulance rushed the infant to the neonatal intensive care unit at St. Mary's Hospital in Knoxville, Tennessee. The days inched by. The little girl got worse. The pediatric specialist regretfully had to tell the parents, "There is very little hope. Be prepared for the worst."

Karen and her husband contacted a local cemetery about a burial plot. They had fixed up a special room in their home for the new baby, but now they found themselves having to plan for a funeral.

Michael, however, kept begging his parents to let him see his sister. "I want to sing to her," he kept saying. Week two in intensive care looked as if a funeral would come before the week was over. Michael kept nagging about singing to his sister, but kids are never allowed in the intensive care unit. Karen made up her mind, though. She would take Michael whether they liked it or not! If he didn't see his sister right then, he may never see her alive.

She dressed him in an oversized scrub suit and marched him into ICU. He looked like a walking laundry basket, but the head nurse recognized him as a child and bellowed, "Get that kid out of here now! No children are allowed!" The mother rose up strong in Karen, and the usually mild-mannered woman glared steel-eyed right into the head nurse's face, her lips a firm line. "He is not leaving until he sings to his sister!"

Karen towed Michael to his sister's bedside. He gazed at the tiny infant losing the battle to live. After a moment, he began to sing. In the pure-hearted voice of a three-year-old, Michael sang: "You are my sunshine, my only sunshine, you make me happy when skies are gray."

Instantly, the baby girl seemed to respond. Her pulse rate began to calm down and become steady. "Keep on singing, Michael," encouraged Karen with tears in her eyes. "You'll never know, dear, how much I love you. Please don't take my sunshine away."

As Michael sang to his sister, the baby's ragged, strained breathing became as smooth as a kitten's purr. "Keep on singing, sweetheart!"

"The other night, dear, as I lay sleeping, I dreamed I held you in my arms…" Michael's little sister began to relax and rest, a healing rest that seemed to sweep over her.

"Keep on singing, Michael." Tears had now conquered the face of the bossy head nurse. Karen glowed. "You are my sunshine, my only sunshine. Please don't take my sunshine away."

The next day - the very next day - the little girl was well enough to go home! Woman's Day magazine called it "The Miracle of a Brother's Song." The medical staff just called it a miracle. Karen called it a miracle of God's love! To the world, you may be one person, but to one person, you may be the world.

True Nobility

A KING SENT word into the village that he was in search of a new court counselor and confidant. The first subject was escorted in and the king inquired what he had done. The man knelt and rattled off his résumé as an architect and mathematician who had designed the castle and the bridge with complicated statistics, plans, and logic. He claimed he could counsel the king on how and why we do what we do.

The second subject was announced and the king inquired of his qualifications. The man knelt and explained that he was the one who had built the castle and the bridge. He could counsel the king and his people on the necessity of having a firm foundation and strong pillars to support them in everything they do.

The third subject was brought in, and the king asked what he had done to qualify for the king's court. He knelt and bragged about his legal and medical degrees. He said he could obviously counsel the king on what was broken and how to fix it.

Distraught and disgusted with the egos and self-centered attitudes of each of them, the king reluctantly invited in the final subject. When he saw an old white haired woman enter the room, he lost his patience and sarcastically inquired what she could have possibly done. Quietly she answered, "I was their teacher."

In response to this, the king rose, stepped down from his throne, and humbly knelt at her feet to pay tribute to the noblest profession of all. For kings and for his subjects, teaching is the profession that makes all other professions possible!

Mathematical Love

We have all taken mandatory classes in school that seemed completely irrelevant to us. For example, in middle school I couldn't see how studying math could possibly help me become a professional football player. At the same time I got my first kiss from my new girlfriend and was focused on finding the formula that would guarantee I could get another one. Then one day it dawned on me. Mathematics is important. In fact, the sooner that I learned math, the sooner I could start applying it to my every day life including getting this next kiss, which was so important to me! This poem describes what happened as I used mathematics to accomplish my goal. I'm sure every guy and father can relate!

Mathematical Love
(Copyright Dan Clark 1982)

He's teaching her arithmetic he said it was his mission
He kissed her once, he kissed her twice, and said,
"Now that's addition"
And as he added smack by smack in silent satisfaction
She sweetly gave the kisses back and said,
"Now that's subtraction"

Then he kissed her, she kissed him,
without an explanation
Then both together smiled and said,
"That's multiplication"
Then dad appeared upon the scene
and made a quick decision
He kicked that kid three blocks away and said,
"That's long division!"

Positive Thinking

2 + 2 = 4. Whether you think positive or negative, the answer is the same. Right? Not according to George.

One morning in 1939 while he was a graduate student at the University of California Berkeley, George Dantzig was late to class and missed the explanation of the statistics professor Jerzy Neyman, who had written two examples of famously unsolved statistics problems on the chalkboard. When Dantzig arrived, he assumed that the two problems were a homework assignment and wrote them down. According to Dantzig, the problems "seemed to be a little harder than usual", but a few days later he handed in completed solutions for the two problems, still believing that they were an assignment that was overdue.

Six weeks later, a knock came at Dantzig's door. He answered and found his excited and overwhelmed statistics professor yelling, "George, George, you've made mathematics history! You missed my explanation before class that we shouldn't worry if we can't solve all the problems. Some are impossible to solve. Not even Einstein could solve them. I put two of them on the board. George, you solved the two most famous unsolved problems in the history of the study of statistics! How did you do it?"

George pondered for a minute and then explained, "If I had heard your explanation that the problems were impossible, do you think I would have even tried to solve them? No way. But with a positive attitude, I attacked the problems and the solutions finally came!"

(This true story has persisted in the form of an urban legend, which even became the introductory scene in the movie Good Will Hunting.)

Positive Discipline

IN MY SOPHOMORE year of high school (Grade 10), I met the anthropology teacher, Mr. Croft. I was a tall, gangly, insecure kid who only went to class to stay eligible for athletic competition. I didn't know anything about anthropology except that "we came from the goo, went through the zoo, and now we're you, whoop-dee-doo," so I never signed up for Mr. Croft's class. The intriguing thing about this is that it didn't stop him from positively impacting my life.

Mr. Croft was a teacher twenty-four hours a day—in the grocery store on Saturday, in the park on Sunday afternoon, after school, before school, and in and out of his classroom. In fact, after graduation I continued to seek out Mr. Croft for counsel and insight.

One day during a visit we were discussing mutual respect and support in the context of positive discipline. I was looking for a firsthand experience from the world of education that would apply to parenting, coaching, and the corporate world of management, sales, and customer service. The conversation centered on how to motivate, inspire, and empower others—not only to increase performance and productivity, but to keep the rules and show respect.

Mr. Croft asked for my definitions. With regard to mutual respect and support, I said, "The only place from which a person can grow is where he or she is."

For positive discipline, I said, "You cannot increase a person's performance by making him or her feel worse; humiliation immobilizes behavior."

Mr. Croft's eyes lit up with excitement as he shared the following experience to illustrate his point. "I had a student who disrupted everything," he said.

"Did you send him to the office?" I asked.

With an offended look on his face, he said, "I've taught school for more than twenty-five years, and I've never sent a student to the principal." Mr. Croft laughed. "Most of my colleagues think the principal has all the Band-Aids. No way. Teachers are responsible for their classrooms and the development and education of each kid. You don't just throw them out when they do something wrong. We have to invite them to grow. We must catch them doing something right."

"Mr. Croft," I interrupted, "I've been to schools where a long line of students trails out the principal's office, down the hall, out the door, and past the 9A bus stop. They're suntanned! And they just stand there with that look of 'Yep, I put a goldfish into the pencil sharpener four months ago, and I'm still waiting to see the principal.' If this is education, we're fooling ourselves! So what did you do with your student?" I asked.

"Interesting you should ask," he replied. "I didn't give up on him. My research uncovered that this James character played in a rock-and-roll band and that he was playing that Friday night in a smoke-filled, honky-tonk, redneck biker bar out in the bushes somewhere. I talked five teachers into going with me so I wouldn't be stabbed all by myself."

"Then what happened?" I asked expectantly.

"Now picture this," Mr. Croft continued. "Six of us in argyle sweaters with matching socks stood at the back of the dance floor surrounded by teenagers who looked like they'd been mugged with a staple gun. The lead singer had a carburetor stuck in his nose. When James spotted us, he leaned into the microphone and asked, 'What are you proctologist-looking teachers doing here?' We told him we heard his band was awesome and wanted to check them out."

Mr. Croft and his colleagues only stayed fifteen minutes. That's all the noise they could take. That was Friday night. On Monday morning, was James a discipline problem in Mr. Croft's class? No way. Was he a problem in Mr. Croft's class the rest of the school year? No way! Was James a discipline problem in other teachers' classrooms for the rest of the school year? Yes! Was it because they couldn't teach? No. It was simply because they didn't care.

An Educational System

MR. CROFT WAS an amazing educator who inspired and taught every student at East High School, especially me. How could I possibly repay him?

A few years after I graduated from high school, I had an opportunity to coach Pop Warner football for thirteen-year-olds who had never played before. To get a feel for the boys' abilities, I lined them up into two lines and had each of them run out for a pass. I wanted to see who could run, catch, and throw so I could formulate a team in my mind.

Two days into practice, a tall, gangly, insecure kid wearing a new shirt, new jeans, and new loafers showed up on the field. I asked him if he didn't want to go home and change his clothes. He boldly replied, "I've already missed two days of practice, and I don't want to miss anymore. I came to play ball!"

He got in line, and when he ran out for a pass, I threw the ball. It hit him square in the head. He picked up the ball and ran it back to me. He slapped it into my chest and ran to the other line. It came time for his second pass and I hit him in the head again. With his nose bleeding and his lip swelling, he picked up the ball, raced it back to me, and got back in line.

On his third attempt, I lofted a soft, easy pass, but it was over his head. He dove for the ball, but came up nowhere near it. Covered with grass stains from head to toe, his body messy, mucky, and soaking wet, he got up, took the muddy ball, raced back to me, and slapped it to my chest.

Figuring I'd better have a chat with him before he killed himself, I pulled him out of line and asked, "Why are you here? Does your dad want you to be a football star? Did your friends talk you into it?"

He looked up with his big brown eyes and said, "Coach, I'm here because I want to play football. And I promise if you'll help me, I know I can do it!"

"What's your name?" I asked.

He shyly answered, "Tommy Croft."

Shocked, I asked if his dad taught anthropology at East High School. Surprised, he replied, "I think so."

"Get back in line," I told him. Here, at last, was my chance to be a Mr. Croft to a Croft! Here was my chance to give something back. For the first time in my life, I understood the meaning of "an educational system." What goes around really does come back around!

Ron

RON GIBBONS WAS a fifteen-year-old teenager, a tenth-grade student at Kearns High School. It was game day, and he was the only sophomore suiting up with the varsity team. Excitedly, he invited his mother to attend. It was her very first football game, and she promised to be there with several of her friends. The game finally ended, and she was waiting outside the locker room to drive Ron home.

"What did you think of the game, Mom? Did you see the three touchdown passes our team made and our tough defense, and the fumble on the kickoff return that we recovered?" he asked.

His mother replied, "Ron, you were magnificent. You have such presence, and I was so pleased with the pride you took in the way you looked. You pulled up your knee socks eleven times during the game, and I could tell you were perspiring in all those bulky pads because you got eight drinks and splashed water on your face twice. I really like how you went out of your way to pat number nineteen, number five and number ninety on the back every time they came off the field."

"Mom, how do you know all that? And how can you say I was magnificent? I didn't even play in the game."

His mother smiled and hugged him. "Ron, I don't know anything about football. I didn't come here to watch the game. I came here to watch you!"

Jillene

HER NAME WAS Jillene Jones. She told me it was Portuguese for "awesome woman" and she was right. She was wonderful! I wanted to go out with her more than anything in the world. I was somewhat insecure and didn't want her to turn me down, so to protect my heart and ego, I asked some of her friends if she would go out with me. They all said yes. I got my confidence up, practiced my voice to make sure it was low and breathy, and phoned her. I asked her to a concert two weeks away. She said yes!

My plan was to get her to fall in love with me. I didn't think Jillene could possibly like me just the way I was, so I started asking around to find out what she did like. I was willing to change anything about myself to get Jillene to fall madly in love with me. I was willing to sell out and compromise my personal authenticity just to reel her in.

I spent the next fourteen days researching Jillene. I discovered her favorite color was peach. What a drag. Peach is a popular color now, but in college it was definitely uncool for a guy to wear peach. You just didn't do it. But it was Jillene's favorite color. I wanted her to fall madly in love with me. Suddenly, it was my favorite color. Interesting how that works, eh? And no, I didn't just buy one peach shirt—I bought five peach shirts. I was thinking long-term relationship!

More research revealed Jillene's favorite men's cologne—an exotic-sounding substance that stunk so bad my nose hairs threatened my life. When I splashed it on, my eyes fogged up, my ears tried to bleed, and my eyes started to sting! But it didn't matter. It was Jillene's favorite cologne. Suddenly it was my favorite cologne. No, I didn't buy the small, date-size bottle. I bought the huge forever- relationship-size bottle. It cost me a bloomin' fortune!

I did more research and discovered Jillene's favorite music. I liked all kinds of music, but hers was really different. Heavy, heavy metal. Brutal loud stuff. Sometimes I think the only reason they call it heavy metal is because the lead singer sounds like he dropped something heavy on his foot! And to think they wrote this all by themselves! Whoa! Give them a Grammy! Yeah, I bought a CD. Suddenly, heavy metal had become my favorite kind of music. It's interesting how insecurity works.

Two weeks went by. It was finally date night. It was time to take Jillene to the concert. I took my research seriously and put on a peach shirt, drenched myself in the cologne, and went to pick up Jillene. I stunk so bad that the flowers on her front porch began to wilt.

Jillene answered the door, and all my preparation paid off. "Oh, my gosh! I can't believe it. Nobody wears peach. Peach is my favorite color." She gave me a hug.

"Oh my gosh," she continued, "this is my favorite smell—my favorite cologne." I coughed and choked, "Me too. I can't believe how many things we have in common." She smiled and said, "I know, I know."

I walked her to the car, opened her door, and walked around the car gagging for oxygen. I then popped in the CD and played her favorite song. As we pulled out of her driveway she leaped over the console and started singing (or screaming) to the beat, and head banging up and down in heavy-metal contortions. I joined her, nodding my head up and down until I accidentally hit her nose on my forehead.

As her nose started to bleed, she yelled, "Wow, you're a great slam dancer. This is my favorite band." I yelled over the loud music, "Me too!" We pulled onto the street and headed for the concert.

Jillene fell madly in love with me exactly as I had planned. In fact, she fell in love with me for two weeks. But something happened. I got sick and tired of being Jillene Jones. I was born to be me! I was born into this world to discover myself and become a unique person that I could love and respect twenty-four hours a day—every day. And yet I had just sold out to win over a woman! And how many women sell out to win over a man? We change our hairstyles, health habits, high expectations, moral standards, style of clothing, cologne, and tastes in music just so an individual or some cliquish group or club will welcome us and accept us with open arms.

After two weeks, I got sick and tired of being Jillene. I was born to be me. So, I gave the peach shirts to my sister. I threw the cologne away. (My trashcans smelled so badly every dog within thirty miles of my home had brain damage!) I then got rid of her musical noise and started listening to my own tunes. I even started doing the old favorite things I had once enjoyed. And do you know what?

It turned out Jillene Jones didn't like that me. When I finally started to be real, we were completely different and she didn't like me. But that's okay because I like me. I have to like and love myself before I can honestly like and love someone else. Do you like and love yourself? If not, why? And if not now, when?

It's What's on the Inside

ON A SPRING day in New York's Central Park, a balloon salesman was busy trying to sell his balloons. In order to gain the attention of those walking in the park, from time to time he would release a brightly colored balloon and let it rise into the sky. On this sunny afternoon, a little African American girl approached him. She was shy and had a poor self-image. She had been watching the man and had a question for him.

"Mister, if you let a black balloon go, will it rise too?"

The balloon salesman knew what the girl was asking. "Sweetheart," he explained. "It doesn't matter what color the balloon is. It's not what's on the outside that makes it rise; it's what's on the inside that makes it go up."

Wild Man

MOST TEACHERS ARE loving, considerate, support-ive, positive individuals. But, as in any profession, there are always negative people who spread negative energy and gossip about others.

Years ago, when I arrived to speak at a high school convocation in Louisiana, I entered the faculty lounge to relax and get my thoughts together. Two teachers stormed through the door and immediately started griping about a student I'll call the Wild Man. "That long-haired, dope-smoking, Frisbee-throwing, skate-board- jumping, flag-burning hippie will never amount to a hill of beans," said one. The other joined in with ridiculous gossip about as accurate as "My wife's sister's dog's mother-in-law told me through the grapevine that he did this and that."

When I couldn't take the negative comments any longer, I found the auditorium and checked out the sound system. There I met the very positive, profes-sional principal who explained the plan for the day.

There was a student in the school who had been a friend to everyone. Zachary was an energetic kid who supported all the games and dances. He had multiple sclerosis—a disease that affects the nerves and muscles.

For years Zach had been in a manual wheelchair, moving from class to class and function to function.

A month before I arrived, Zach's condition worsened and he needed a motorized wheelchair to stay at this school. Without it, he would have to attend a school with special equipment. It turned out that Zach couldn't afford the new electric chair, so his only choice was to check out. Today was the day Zach was leaving; he was in the counselor's office with his parents filling out the final paperwork.

The school assembly was announced and Zach and his parents were casually invited into the auditorium. The students and faculty filled the giant room and Zach took his usual spot out in the aisle on the fifteenth row. Zach assumed it was his last day and last event at this school. Before they introduced me as the speaker, the real drama unfolded.

The student body president was introduced and he came onstage for the Pledge of Allegiance. He then shocked everyone when he introduced Wild Man—the kid the teachers were degrading in the faculty lounge. With green hair, numerous rings in his ear, and two fly-fishing hooks in his eyebrow, Wild Man caused a stir among the teachers.

Without saying a word, Wild Man gave a signal and four football players approached Zach, lifted him out of the wheelchair, and brought him to the center of the stage. Wild Man gave another signal and two students from the band presented Zach's parents with flowers and escorted them to the stage. Wild Man then excused himself and disappeared backstage. Seconds later, he reappeared driving a brand-new, shiny, chrome-plated electric wheelchair with a giant bow in the school colors taped on the side.

Wild Man spun around and stepped out to allow the football players to place Zach in the chair. They showed him how to operate it and moved aside as Zach took two victory laps around the stage. With tears streaming, two thousand students and faculty members simultaneously leaped to their feet to give a five- minute standing ovation.

Were they just cheering for Zach and the fact that he could now remain in their school? No, they were also cheering for Wild Man, who had used his own initiative to rally for Zach's new chair. His mohawked, tattooed, punk-rocker friends had caught wind of his special need and had banded together and collected enough money on their own to buy the chair.

So, it's true: we shouldn't judge a book by its cover. When given a chance to feel wanted, important, capable, and needed, even the most deceiving "books" can deliver a great moral to the story. Remember: "A broken clock is right twice a day." Never give up on anyone!

The Last Game

IT WAS THE last football game of Brian's senior year, and a message came that his father had died. When the coach found out, he decided to tell Brian before the game, knowing he probably would elect not to play. But instead of reacting sorrowfully, Brian just took it all in stride and said, "I'll leave right after the game."

The coach had heard Brian speak highly of his father and expected him to grieve. When he didn't, the coach said, "Brian, you don't have to play. This game isn't that important."

Brian ignored him and played the game anyway. And play he did. Brian was the star, winning the game as a man possessed. In the locker room, the other players showered with Brian. Some offered condolences, but most were appalled at his lack of sorrow. Brian was casual and happy, as if nothing had gone wrong. The coach was angry and worried that he had taught too much devotion to sports and not enough compassion. He scolded Brian, "Why did you play the game? Your father is dead. I'm ashamed of you and of myself."

Brian replied, "Coach, this was our last game. I am a senior. I had to play. This was the first time my dad has ever seen me play, and I had to play like I never played before."

The coach didn't understand. With tears streaming down his cheeks, Brian replied, "You didn't know my father was blind, did you?"

Pay Attention

JASON CAME FROM a good family with two loving parents, two brothers, and a sister. They were all successful academically and socially. They lived in a posh neighborhood. Jason had everything a boy could desire. But he was always into some kind of mischief. He wasn't a bad kid who caused trouble, but he always wound up in the thick of bad things.

In first grade, Jason was labeled Special Ed. They tried to keep him out of the regular classes. In middle school, he was the "misfit troublemaker." In high school, although never officially tested, Jason was tagged with having attention deficit/hyperactivity disorder (ADHD). More often than not, his teachers kicked him out of class. His first report card had one C and all Ds.

One Sunday, the family was enjoying brunch at the country club when a teacher stopped and said, "Jason is doing so well these days. We're pleased and delighted."

"You must be mixing us up with another family," said the father. "Our Jason is worthless. He is always in trouble. We are so embarrassed and just can't figure out why."

As the teacher walked away, the mother remarked, "You know, honey, come to think of it, Jason hasn't been in trouble for a month. He's even been going to school early and staying late. I wonder what's up?"

The second nine-week grading period was finally up. As usual, Jason's mom and dad expected low grades and unsatisfactory marks in behavior. Instead, he achieved four As, three Bs, and honors in citizenship. His parents were baffled.

"Who did you sit by to get these grades?" his dad asked sarcastically. "I did it all myself," Jason humbly answered.

Perplexed, and still not satisfied, the parents took Jason back to school to meet with the principal. He assured them that Jason was doing very well. "We have a new guidance counselor, and she seems to have touched your son in a special way," he said. "His self-esteem is much better, and he's doing great this term. I think you should meet her."

When the trio approached the counselor, the woman had her head down. It took a moment for her to notice she had visitors. When she did, she leaped to her feet and began gesturing with her hands. "What's this?" asked Jason's father indignantly. "Sign language? Why, she can't even hear."

"That's why she's so great," said Jason, jumping in between them. "She does more than hear, Dad. She listens!"

Needed?

A MOTHER SHARED a story about her twenty-year-old son John who was handsome and talented, a good citizen, a good student, a good musician, and a gifted athlete. He also had a lovely girlfriend and seemed to have no problems. One day he stopped talking as much as he usually did.

Thirty days passed, and his conversation dwindled to nothing. He was depressed, and his parents and girlfriend continually told him that they loved him. He knew that they loved him, and he expressed his love for them. Everyone was concerned about his well-being and wondered what they could say or do to help him, since saying, "I love you" obviously wasn't enough to improve the situation.

John finally made a move. He locked himself in the cellar. Although he was down in the dim dampness for three days without food, he continued to acknowledge his parents' love for him and his love for them. But his depression deepened, and his loved ones were convinced suicide was imminent. Healthcare professionals were brought in, but the counseling, kindness, caring, and love did not help.

On the third day of John's isolation, the local high school football coach (who didn't know what was going on in John's life) called his home to talk to him. John's mother said John was busy and took a message at the coach's request. Then she went to the cellar door and called down the stairs, "John, Coach Ivers just phoned.

He said that his players voted last night on who they wanted as their assistant coach. They said you were the greatest Pop Warner football coach they had ever had and now they think they can win the state championship if you help coach them. Coach Ivers said they need you—he needs you! He said if you're interested, you should be at football practice at 2:45 this afternoon."

Do you know what happened? Sure you do! John came out of the cellar and went to practice. He accepted the coaching job, and by the time he came home from his first practice, he had snapped out of his depression. He once again felt needed, wanted, and important, and he was back to his old self.

Painful Preparation

A FEW YEARS ago, I went to a workout session of the University of Utah women's gymnastic team. I learned why they win consistently. Her name was Missy Marlowe, and she eventually competed on the U.S. Olympic gymnastics team in 1988. She was also named one of the prestigious top six—one of the six best male and female athletes in the United States—and received the Broderick Award as the NCAA Outstanding Female Athlete of the Year.

When I first saw her, Missy was a young freshman on the uneven parallel bars, trying to execute a difficult maneuver. I watched her crash to the mat ten times in a row. After the tenth fall, she sobbed and limped away, but it didn't stop her. She came back, and I watched her fall four more times, each time smashing hard into the mat. Finally, on the fifteenth try, Missy spun off the bar, reached out, and completed the maneuver.

Coach Marsden told me afterward that every new girl goes through the same thing to learn each one of the many difficult moves required to win meets and please judges. Nobody clapped that day. There were no cameras to record her victory.

But her face showed personal satisfaction. And when she eventually won the national championship that year in the all-around competition, the hard work, sacrifice, and painful endurance were all worth it.

Would you have quit on the first crash? The tenth? The fourteenth? How many of us would have realized that just one more attempt would make the difference between failure and success? Any great achievement in life requires hours of lonely, deliberate preparation and work. Don't make the mistake of thinking that athletes, artists, doctors, attorneys, writers, or actors didn't spend years learning how to perform in their areas of expertise. You can be sure they paid their dues in time, effort, and solitude. They were convinced, however, that there's no gain without pain. No Pain No Gain really means No Heart No Chance!

A Champion's Discipline

RESPONSIBILITY BRINGS FREEDOM and freedom provides opportunity. That's the principle of self-discipline. Self-discipline sounds like some kind of punishment you administer to yourself. It really means you are in control of your actions and the outcome—at least to some degree.

Self-discipline means avoiding outside discipline by doing the right thing. Arabian horses are a perfect example of the kind of self-control each of us is capable of achieving. These magnificent horses with intelligent eyes, well-formed heads, and flowing manes and tails win many championships because of their stamina and courage.

While they are all hearty specimens, some horses stand above the others for endurance and intelligence. To determine which they are, trainers teach them to drink only when they hear a whistle. Once they have learned to obey, they are placed in a corral under the hot sun until they are parched. Then water is brought and placed outside the corral out of their reach, forcing them to wait even longer.

Finally, a gate is opened, and most of them stampede for the trough to drink with reckless abandon. Only a few stand poised with pride, holding their heads erect, and don't give in to the terrible craving. Only when they hear the whistle do they allow themselves to drink. The ones who obey and resist the urge to drink are reserved for special training. The other steeds are led away.

So it is with humans. The mark of a champion is not on the outside, but somewhere deep inside, where self-control resides. To gain control of your self and become self-disciplined is the second step to becoming successful. First, see yourself as a conqueror. Then discipline yourself to become one. Unfortunately, many folks who see themselves as champions are not willing to put in the extra effort and self-imposed discipline to become winners. Consequently, they lose out to those with restraint.

What Really Makes a Leader?

DURING THE 1968 Special Olympics, a special competition for mentally and physically challenged athletes. Kim Peek was competing in the fifty-yard dash. Kim had been diagnosed with Autism and was racing against two other amazing young people who had been diagnosed with cerebral palsy. They were in wheelchairs and Kim was the lone runner. As the gun sounded, Kim moved quickly ahead. Ten yards from the finish line, he turned to see how the others were doing. One girl had turned her wheelchair around and was stuck against the wall. The other boy was pushing his wheelchair with his feet.

Kim stopped and retraced his steps. He pushed the little girl across the finish line. Meanwhile, the boy going backward won the race. The girl took second and Kim lost. Or did he?

The greatest leader and champion does not always win the race but gains honor and recognition by serving others.

He Who Travels the Road Best

ONCE UPON A time, a king had a great highway built. Before he opened it to the public, he had a contest to see who could travel the highway best. On the appointed day, the people came. Some had fine chariots; some used their feet. But no matter what vehicle they used, all of them complained that there was a large pile of rocks on the side of the road in one particular spot that hindered their progress.

At the end of the day, a lone traveler crossed the finish line and wearily walked over to the king. He was smudged with dirt, but he spoke with respect as he handed the monarch a bag of gold.

"I stopped along the way to clear a pile of rocks," he said. "And under it was a bag of gold. Can you find the rightful owner?"

Solemnly, the king replied, "You are the rightful owner. You have earned the gold by winning the contest. For he who travels the road best is he who makes the road smoother for those who follow."

So it is in life. While people scramble to outdo each other, every now and then a leader comes along to pave the way for the rest of us. To these leaders are given the rewards, the sacks of gold called gratitude, love, admiration, respect, and confirmation that their lives mattered. And FYI – you never want to burn a bridge because you never know how many times you are going to need to cross the river!

Never Say Never

RICHARD NELSON, A sixteen-year-old junior at Manti High School in Utah, was an outstanding athlete. He was the number-two singles player on the state championship tennis team and had just made the basketball team that would go on that year to win the state championship. He was looking forward to much success as a senior during the following season. But on October 23, 1966, most of his athletic future was suddenly taken away from him.

That night, Richard was riding his bicycle from Manti to Gunnison to visit his girlfriend. The road was very steep in some places, which allowed Richard to reach speeds of forty miles per hour on the downhill slopes. Because it was dark and difficult to see, Richard was following the white line on the shoulder of the road to ensure his safety. As he came around a blind curve and was looking down at the ground, Richard failed to see a parked car jacked up to fix a flat tire on his side of the road. With no warning, he hit the parked car and ended up in the hospital, where he didn't regain consciousness for two days.

Besides bad cuts on his head and knee, he broke his collarbone and right arm. He wore an L-shaped cast on his arm for two months. When the cast came off on December 29, Richard's doctor gave him a series of tests to determine the success of his healing. Richard failed all the tests. His triceps muscle had lost all its strength—he could not push out with his arm. The doctor diagnosed a pinched nerve and said that Richard might never regain the use of his right arm. Richard's once strong but now puny right arm just hung at his side, and the doctor gave him no real hope of recovery.

Because of his injury, Richard wasn't able to play on the basketball team during the rest of that year, but the coach made him equipment and statistics manager so that he could come to practice and be around the guys on the team.

His junior year ended, the summer came, and Richard was determined to do whatever he had to do to make the basketball team the next year. He realized that he couldn't make it right-handed, so he started working on his left-handed skills.

All summer long, each and every night, he practiced making left-handed baskets at the outdoor courts in the center of town. Every night, he shot two hundred left- handed baskets and practiced left-handed dribbling and passing off the park retaining wall. Instead of going with his friends to the summer dances sponsored by the high school, Richard practiced basketball.

When the next season arrived, Richard was ready to try out for the team—and he made it! He never became a starter but he was always the first substitute to go in the game.

The season boiled down to the final game of the year against their archrival, Richfield High. This game would determine which team would win the league championship and advance to the state tournament playoffs. It was a "must win" for both teams.

On Friday night, the gym was packed. The starting guard for Manti had sprained his ankle earlier in the week, so Richard finally got his big break—he started the game! However, before the first quarter was over, Richard was replaced. It was hard to compete when he could only use one arm.

The game continued until the last thirty seconds when Manti's other guard was injured, forcing Richard back into the game. Richfield was ahead by three points, and Manti had the ball. The Richfield team's coach tried to take advantage of the situation by having one of his players immediately foul Richard. Undaunted, Richard stepped up to the free throw line. (If he made the first foul shot, he would get a chance to shoot and make a second basket.)

Confidently, Richard picked up the ball, braced it in his left hand, and shot. Swish! He made it, and the crowd went wild! He then made the next shot, bringing Manti High to within one point of Richfield. The crowd stood and went crazy again!

Richfield then took the ball out of bounds and threw a long pass down court to the player Richard was guarding, trying to make a quick, easy basket. But Richard, with his undying determination, leaped through the air to intercept the pass. When he landed he was fouled again, and was given another opportunity at the free throw line. With ten seconds left on the clock, Richard balanced the ball in his left hand, took a deep breath, and shot. The crowd was deathly quiet until— swish! He tied the game! His next shot went up, down and through. Swish again!

He made it—he made all four shots—left-handed! Richard Nelson won the game and became the hero of the school. According to Richard, he was not a hero. "Anybody could have done what I did," he said in his postgame interview. "I was supposed to make those shots. Everybody was counting on me to win the game when I was put in that situation. All I did was believe in myself, work hard when others didn't, and persevere.

Anybody could have done what I did in the game if they had shot as many foul shots as I had shot last summer in practice." As Earl Nightingale said, "The only difference between a successful person and an unsuccessful person is that the successful person will do what the unsuccessful person will not do. The key is the successful person does not want to do it either, but then does it anyway."

Winning Isn't Beating Someone

A FRIEND OF mine experienced a miracle in a Mesa, Arizona, school that caters to learning disabled children. Randy Gray's young boy diligently does everything he can to learn and grow in strength. Every day, Randy stops by the school after work so the two of them can walk home together.

One afternoon, they walked past a park where some young men the boy knew were playing baseball. The boy asked, "Do you think they will let me play?" His father knew that his son was not athletic, and because of his disabilities, most boys would not want him on their team. But his father understood that if his son was allowed to play, it would give him a much-needed sense of belonging.

The boy's father approached one of the young men and asked if his son could play. The boy looked around for guidance from his teammates. Getting none, he took matters into his own hands and said, "We're losing by six runs, and the game is in the eighth inning. I guess he can be on our team and we'll try to put him up to bat in the ninth inning." The father was ecstatic as his son smiled broadly.

In the bottom on the eighth inning, the losing team scored a few runs but was still behind by three. In the bottom of the ninth, the boy's team scored again, and now with two outs and the bases loaded, with the potential winning run on base, Randy's son was scheduled to be up to bat. Would the team actually let him bat at this juncture and give away their chance to win the game?

Surprisingly, the boy was given the bat. Everyone knew he was mentally and physically challenged. The boy didn't even know how to hold the bat properly, let alone hit. However, as he stepped up to the plate, the pitcher moved up a few steps to lob the ball in softly so he could at least make contact. The first pitch came in and the boy swung clumsily and missed.

One of his teammates ran to him, and together they held the bat and faced the pitcher, waiting for the next throw. The pitcher again took a few steps forward to toss the ball softly toward the determined little boy. As the pitch came in, he and his teammate swung the bat, and together they hit a slow ground ball to the pitcher.

The pitcher picked up the soft grounder and could easily have thrown the ball to the first baseman. The little boy would have been out by a mile, and that would have ended the game. Instead, the pitcher took the ball and threw it on a high arc to right field, far beyond reach of the first baseman. Everyone started yelling, "Run, buddy, run to first. Run to first!" Never in his life had the boy run to first.

He scampered and limped down the baseline wide-eyed and startled. By the time he reached first base, the right fielder had the ball. He could have thrown the ball to the second baseman who would have tagged him out, but the right fielder understood what the pitcher's intentions were, so he threw the ball high and far over the third baseman's head. Everyone yelled, "Run to second, run to second."

Again, startled, but with a grin on his face so big he could have eaten a banana sideways, the little guy ran. As he reached second base, the opposing shortstop ran to him, turned him in the direction of third base, and shouted, "Run to third." As he rounded third, the nine boys from each team ran behind him screaming, "Run, little buddy, run home!"

He ran home and stepped on home plate. All eighteen boys from both teams lifted him on their shoulders and made him the hero. He had just hit a "grand slam" and won the game for his team!

With tears rolling down his face, Randy softly whispered, "I witnessed a real miracle that day. Not only did those eighteen boys realize the power of empathy, compassion, and service above self, but they let a father and his struggling son share together the power of a dream and the power of emotional connection that comes only through the magic of unconditional love!"

Look Hard Before
You Leave Home

IN THE MIDDLE 1800s there was a gold rush in America. One man got so excited that he sold his ranch in northern California to move to southern California to look for gold. He sold his home to a former army colonel and never came back. The colonel put a mill on a stream that ran through the property. One day his little girl brought home some sand from the stream in a jar, and she sifted through it. In the sand were the first shining nuggets of gold that were discovered in California. The man who had owned the ranch wanted gold. If he had stayed on his land, he could have secured all the gold he ever dreamed of. Since that day, thirty-eight million dollars worth of gold has been taken out of the land he sold, a stark reminder to all of us that we should always look before we leave!

You Can if You Think You Can

IN DECEMBER 1982, my dear friend Bob Coyne of Brantford, Ontario, decided to host a junior hockey team from Sweden. In exchange, the members of Bob's Canadian junior team would travel to Sweden the following year as guests of the Swedish team. The team from Sweden arrived in Canada on Boxing Day (December 26). This team was the pride and joy of Stockholm. It consisted of fourteen and 15-year old boys, handpicked from Stockholm and its vicinity, and was reputed to be a notoriously tough hockey club. As hosts, Bob and his team were to provide the Swedish team with a tour of each of the seven different communities where it would play its seven exhibition games. The final game was to be between the Stockholm team and Bob's Brantford team.

Upon arriving in Canada, the Stockholm team's hope, of course, was to win all seven games and return home with grand tales of victory. It was the first time away from home for these kids. They were suffering from jet lag, and they lost their first game by a dismal 8–1 score. It was a staggering defeat for them. They were a little more prepared for the second game, but again they lost, this time 4–2. They lost the third and fourth games as well. The fifth game was a devastating 9–1 lashing.

At this point in the tour, which was somewhere around New Year's Day, Bob decided they needed a break in the action, a diversion to rally their confidence and rebuild their self-esteem. He arranged a visit to Toronto to see the CN Tower, the National Hockey League Hall of Fame, and other points of interest. The Swedish team would play no hockey for two entire days, but could swim and play basketball at a local high school for entertainment and exercise.

At the end of the Toronto trip, Bob took them to the student center to sit and relax while they waited for the bus to pick them up and take them back to their sponsoring homes. The coach of the Stockholm team asked Bob if there was something he could say to his team that might psych them up for the next game. Bob was neither prepared nor thinking in those terms, but he decided, on the spur of the moment, to see if he could touch their emotions.

Bob started talking to them about home, which got them right up off their chairs. He asked them if they missed their moms and dads and if the time change was bothering them. Bob explained that in Stockholm, there were fewer daylight hours during the winter than there were in Canada, and surely this change was affecting them.

Bob finally steered the conversation toward hockey, reflecting on their five losses in a row, which surely was not typical of the team, and how they all must feel about these losses. Bob concluded by suggesting that what they needed was something to which they could reach out and relate. He told them that all they needed was the confidence to believe in themselves again. So he left them with a phrase he had heard many other times: "You can if you think you can."

Bob then repeated this phrase to each kid individually while he looked each one squarely in the eye. When he had repeated the phrase to each one of them, he left the room. A few moments later, the bus arrived and they all left. Bob really didn't think he had convinced them, but he went home prepared to reinforce the idea anyway. He made a big sign bearing the phrase YOU CAN IF YOU THINK YOU CAN and took it with him to the next game, which was held at the Six Nations Indian Reservation just south of Francis. Six Nations had a top-notch hockey club, and the Stockholm team knew it. Even prior to arriving in Canada, the Stockholm team was prepared that if it lost a game, it would be either go to Six Nations or to Brantford.

Game time arrived, and the Swedish team was still in the locker room. They didn't appear to be coming out, so Bob went in to see what was happening. Most of the team members hung their heads while their coach addressed them, and Bob could see they just weren't up for the game. They turned to look at Bob when he barged in. He smiled broadly and said, "Remember, you can if you think you can!" He waved to the Swedish coach and swiftly exited the locker room.

Bob then hung the sign he had made, unbeknownst to the Swedish team, on the back of their team bench. A minute later, the Swedish team emerged and saw the sign. Spontaneously, every member of the team touched the sign. From there, they went out onto the ice, warmed up, and then faced off to open the game.

Very early on, they took a 1–0 lead, and again they all jumped the boards, touched the sign, and went back out for the face-off. The game continued. The Swedish team scored another goal and again, each member of the team touched the sign. Six Nations came back to tie the game, but for those kids who hadn't won a single game during their entire tour, the tie was as good as a win. The tie put them on top of the world. The noise during the bus ride home was unbelievable!

That brings us to the last day of the tournament. Bob's Brantford team was the Stockholm team's last opponent. He had arranged to pick up the Stockholm team's coach at his hotel room for a pregame lunch. When Bob entered the coach's room, he saw the YOU CAN IF YOU THINK YOU CAN sign propped up on the headboard of the bed. Bob thought it was kind of funny, but he could see that the Stockholm coach really believed it because, as they left for the arena, he grabbed the sign to hang over the bench.

When the Swedish team came onto the ice, they performed the same ritual as they had at Six Nations, each player touched the sign before the start of the game. This final game of the series was a highly competitive, spirited contest and Stockholm beat Brantford by two points. Every time the Swedish team scored, they touched the sign and also skated past Bob's bench grinning and triumphantly shaking their fists at him. There was a party for the team after the game ended, and the next morning, the players flew home to Stockholm.

The following December, Bob's team arrived in Stockholm for the exchange tournament. The setup for sports in Sweden is different from the setup in Canada. The Swedes have sports clubs for almost every sport, but all the clubs play in the same arena. The sports building is in downtown Stockholm, and Bob and his junior team went there for a reception following their arrival in Sweden. As they entered the main lobby of the huge, city-owned, government-operated arena, Bob noticed the YOU CAN IF YOU THINK YOU CAN sign hanging on the wall about twelve feet from the floor. The sign was framed, and beneath it was an inscription of the story of its origin and impact. Bob was surprised, happy, and choked up all at the same time.

To this day, that sign still graces the lobby of the Stockholm sports complex, teaching the value of the power of positive thinking to all who enter!

Questions and Answers

MY COLLEGE PROFESSOR asked his students to list what we thought were the Seven Wonders of the World. Out of the hundred students in the lecture hall, the general consensus was:

1. Pyramids of Egypt
2. Great Wall of China
3. Grand Canyon
4. Taj Mahal
5. Rainbow Bridge
6. Stonehenge
7. Golden Gate Bridge

While gathering the votes, the professor noted that one student had not yet finished her paper. He asked the girl if she was having trouble answering the question. She replied, "No, I'm not having trouble with the answer; I'm having trouble with the question. Why only seven? According to whom and what criteria? What does 'wonder' mean to you, and is it different for me?"

The professor responded, "Tell us what you have, and maybe we can help." The girl hesitated and then read, "I think the real Seven Wonders of the World are to see, to hear, to taste, to touch, to laugh, to feel, and to love."

The room was so quiet you could have heard a pin drop. The professor took a deep breath and replied, "Wow! This is the most profound lesson we will learn all year. And isn't it pathetic that out of the 101 people in this room—me included—that only one of us, only 1 percent, understands that the things we overlook as simple and fundamental truly are wondrous?"

This story provides four powerful reminders: The most important and precious things in life cannot be bought or built by hand; Before we look for answers outside of ourselves, let us first look within; Life is not about answers; it's about questions; Oftentimes we need to also question the answers.

Overcoming

AT AGE FOURTEEN, Michael Dowling fell from the back of a wagon in a blizzard. Before his parents realized it and returned to find him, he had been severely frostbitten. Both of his legs had to be amputated, one at the hip, the other at the knee. His right arm and left hand were amputated as well. When he came out of surgery and examined what was left of his body, Michael was so depressed he said he wanted to commit suicide, but he couldn't figure out how to do it.

Over time, he snapped out of it and went to the board of county commissioners and told them if they would buy him some artificial limbs and educate him, he would pay them back in full. They fulfilled his request.

Years later, during World War II, the army sent Michael to Europe to visit wounded soldiers. Standing in a hotel, he spoke to a large group of bedridden men that had lost an eye, a leg, or an arm. He began to minimize the seriousness of their wounds, and the soldiers were getting upset. In fact, they began to boo him. In response, Michael began to walk toward them and told them to set high goals for themselves and not to feel sorry for themselves. The enraged soldiers then yelled obscenities at him.

Finally, he sat down on a chair and took off his right leg. The soldiers calmed down a bit, but they still resented him. Then he took off his left leg. The booing stopped but Michael didn't. He took off his right arm, flipped off his left hand, and there he sat, a stump of a body. Now that he had their attention, Dowling delivered a speech on taking personal responsibility for success through goal setting and turning lemons into lemonade.

You see, Michael Dowling had become the president of one of the largest banks in Minnesota, a father of five, and the U.S. Chamber of Commerce Man of the Year.

When Your Attitude Is Right

It was the third game of Danny's sophomore year. His University of Utah football team had not yet won a game, and they had just been beaten by more than twenty points by a much-inferior, last-place team. It was the day after the game and Danny's team was assembled in the meeting room watching the game films of the embarrassing loss. Suddenly the coach yelled, "Stop the projector. Run that play again."

To the team, the play was not that impressive. The opposing team's running back got the ball and ran around the end with a Utah player coming up and hitting him hard. The Utah player bounced off their guy who continued to run down the field for an additional twenty-five yards before he was finally tackled from behind.

This play impressed the Utah coach so much that he rewound and watched the play seven times in a row. He finally said, "Turn off the projector, turn on the lights, and listen to what I'm about to teach you. It appears to me that only one player on our team understands the key to winning success. When our guy Danny came up and hit their guy, it was obvious in the film that Danny bounced off and missed the tackle!

But Danny was the same guy who tackled their guy twenty-five yards down the field. Danny wasn't even supposed to play or see any action. He was third string on the depth chart. But when the first two players ahead of him got injured, Danny was put in the game. From now on, Danny will start every game. He is my kind of guy. You see, Danny's attitude is right. And when your attitude is right, your abilities will always catch up!"

Get Yourself Right

A FATHER CAME home from work one afternoon and his son wanted him to spend some time playing with him. The father knew he had work he had to get done that couldn't wait. The son was very insistent, and the father had to come up with something to keep the young boy occupied.

On the coffee table lay a magazine that contained a map of the world. The father ripped the map into numerous tiny pieces, gave the pieces to his young son, and instructed him to go put the map back together. The son left the room and the father got to work, thinking it would take a number of hours for the son to put the puzzle together.

To his surprise, just fifteen minutes later, the son was back and the puzzle was assembled. Amazed, the father asked how he finished so quickly. "It was easy. On the other side of the map was a picture of a man. When I got the man right, the whole world was right!"

Together We Can Make It

BOB BUTLER LOST his legs in a 1965 land mine explosion in Vietnam. He returned home a war hero. Twenty years later, he proved once again that heroism comes from the heart. Butler was working in his garage in a small town in Arizona on a hot summer day when he heard a woman's screams coming from a nearby house. He began rolling his wheelchair toward the house, but the dense shrubbery wouldn't allow him access to the back door. So he got out of his chair and started to crawl through the dirt and bushes.

"I had to get there," he said. "It didn't matter how much it hurt." When Butler arrived at the pool, there was a three-year-old girl named Stephanie Hanes lying at the bottom. She had been born without arms and had fallen into the water and couldn't swim. Her mother stood over her baby, screaming frantically. Butler dove to the bottom of the pool and brought little Stephanie up to the deck. Her face was blue, she had no pulse, and she was not breathing.

Butler immediately went to work performing CPR to revive her while Stephanie's mother telephoned the fire department. She was told that the paramedics were already out on a call. Helplessly, she sobbed and hugged Butler's shoulder. As Butler continued with his CPR, he calmly reassured her. "Don't worry," he said. "I was her arms to get out of the pool. It'll be okay. I am now her lungs. Together we can make it."

Seconds later the little girl coughed, regained consciousness, and began to cry. As they hugged and rejoiced together, the mother asked Butler how he knew it would be okay. "When my legs were blown off in the war, I was all alone in a field," he told her. "No one was there to help except a little Vietnamese girl. As she struggled to drag me into her village, she whispered in broken English, 'It okay. You can live. I be your legs. Together we make it.'" He told the mother that this was his chance to return the favor.

Bird Talk

HAVE YOU EVER tried to teach a bird to talk? I bought a parakeet and promptly started the process. I looked the bird in the eye and said, "Danny, Danny," over and over again. Fifty repetitions a day for two straight months! A total of three thousand repetitions. Then it finally happened. One morning as I was leaving the room, the parakeet blurted out, "Danny."

Now it was time to teach him his last name, Clark. I followed the same process: "Clark, Clark." It only took two hundred repetitions over a week, and the bird finally said, "Clark." The learning process curve was speeding up! Then something very interesting happened. I got sick and spent two days in the house coughing and coughing.

That weekend, I had a party. When I showed off my talking bird, I discovered a great principle about why we do the things we do. Positive or negative, we learned it all the same way. I got the bird's attention and it said "Danny Clark. Cough!" Yes, the bird coughed.

Now, did I teach the bird to cough? No! The bird was a product of its environment, and so are human beings. What goes into our minds stays and will eventually come back out. How did we learn to talk and walk and sing and dance? We are not born—we are made. With the right input, we can actually become the "bird" we dream to be!

Piano Perfection

WHEN ERNEST SAUNDERS was a sixteen-year-old high school student in Philadelphia, he was taken by his music teacher to a scholarship audition at the world famous Settlement Music School. He took his place at the piano and began to play a complicated concerto. Suddenly, Mrs. Evans, the school official, stood up and applauded and awarded Ernest a full scholarship. He was to enroll immediately.

Mrs. Evans was astounded at his ability and said his talent and playing grace were truly magnificent. With tears streaming down her cheeks, Mrs. Evans rushed forward to finish seeing and hearing Ernest brilliantly play the classical piece. Why?

He was born with only one finger on his right hand. Ernest has gone on to record several critically acclaimed albums and is one of the great entertainers, teachers, and modern composers of our time. How? Why?

Each day, his students see a Bernard Edmonds quote hanging above his desk that answers all inquiries: "To dream anything that you want to dream. That is the beauty of the human mind. To do anything that you want to do. That is the strength of the human will. To trust yourself to test your limits. That is the courage to succeed!"

Attention!

THE OCCASION WAS the state high school conference for the Texans' War on Drugs. The setting was a high school gymnasium crammed with more than two thousand teenagers waiting for the opening general session to begin. A young man strolled up to the stage, stood on one foot with his left elbow resting on the podium, put his right hand on his stomach, and casually began to recite the Pledge of Allegiance.

Suddenly a tall, dark-haired man rose from his chair on the stage. It was apparent that he was the director of the organization presiding over this event. The man walked to the podium and interrupted the young man's recitation.

"My name is General Robinson Risner. I was the highest-ranking prisoner of war in the Vietnam War. I spent seven years locked up in solitary confinement. My fellow military service men and I were tortured beyond belief. Our limbs were dislocated, we were beat to a pulp at least once a week, and I limp because of this horrifying experience. Today I still have a hole in the front of my skull from the Chinese water torture inflicted on me.

However, I willingly and proudly gave up years of my life away from my beloved family and friends defending our flag and our country and all the sacred and wonderful principles that they represent. America is the greatest country on the planet, the international leader of human rights, and of the free world. And you should show this country and her flag abiding respect. Hundreds of thousands of American soldiers have died for this flag. This young man's attitude toward our flag and country today are a disgrace to everything we hold dear—especially to the very freedom that allows us to gather here today. Therefore, let's do this again."

General Risner continued, "When we say the Pledge of Allegiance, we stand at attention. We place our right hands over our hearts, we look directly at the flag, and we say the words with conviction and pride. Please join me." A respectful silence filled the room. He then recited the Pledge in a way that I had never before heard—in a way that touched my life forever—in a way that taught everyone present the true meaning of patriotism, duty, honor, and country.

It's been many years since that significant experience, yet every time I see an American flag, and every time I stand for the National Anthem I vividly remember it. The flag is more than colored cloth. The Star Spangled Banner is more than just a song! They symbolize everything for which America stands—every little thing and every single person that has ever contributed to making America great.

Flag-burners and disrespectful leaders young and old, who flippantly mouth the words of our pledge or refuse to stand for our National Anthem should rethink their actions. You can be anti-war, anti-Democrat, anti-Republican, anti-guns, or anti-abortion—but don't ever be anti-American. The flag is not a symbol of any special interest group, political or social faction, racial group, or sexual preference. The flag is the symbol of a free republic and democratic society wherein we can all celebrate our differences, and more important, be free to do so. The flag is what binds us together. The flag is part of you and it is part of me, and it waves for all the world to see everything we have the opportunity to be. Standing at attention for our flag is key. Show some dignity!

Seat To A Soldier

IT'S NOT ENOUGH to shake the hand of a man or woman in military uniform and say thanks. Our troops have been at war for nineteen years while we've been at the mall! It's not enough to put a magnetic sign on the side of our vehicles that says "Support Our Troops" and feel like we're doing our part. That's why I made a commitment many years ago that whenever I saw a soldier, airman, sailor, or marine in an airport, I would buy him or her a meal. What a drag! No one told me they don't hang out by themselves. They're always in groups of three, five, ten. I'm going broke!

Because winning isn't a sometime thing, it's an all-the-time thing, and because service before self is a governing core value that we don't turn off and on, I also needed to take this same commitment on board my flights. I always fly first class (Delta Airlines takes great care of me), and I always get a window seat. One day I was seated, drinks had been served, and the other passengers started to board the plane. As the slower moving people caused congestion in the aisle, a soldier in his combat uniform was stopped at my row. So, I chatted him up. "How are you?"

"I'm fine, Sir."

"Are you coming or going?"

"I'm coming back from the desert, Sir."

They are always so polite. I said, "I bet you are excited to see your family."

He said, "Yes, Sir, I've been in Iraq for fifteen months, and I hope they are excited to see me."

I said, "Guaranteed, bro! Welcome home," and offered him my seat. He replied, "No, thank you, Sir, that's not necessary."

I said, "What do you mean it's not necessary? It's the least I can do. C'mon, swap seats with me." I stood up and he reluctantly slid in to sit down. The flight attendant acknowledged how cool she thought this was, to which I responded that it was the least any of us could do and to take good care of him and give him anything he wants.

As I moved to the back of the plane to find his seat, wouldn't you know it? He had a middle seat between two chubby guys. I'm six foot five and weigh 235 pounds! Both guys were looking at me like, "Oh no!" I was wincing back "Oh, yes."

As I sat down and squished my body in between them, it was easy to feel sorry for myself. It was a four hour flight and this was not what I had in mind. I felt like I had sat on a stick and my immediate discomfort flipped my positive commitment to service before self to a self-centered negative focus on what was wrong.

I silently complained, "I'm so old that I bend over to pull up my socks and think, what else can I accomplish while I'm way down here?" I go to bed healthy and wake up injured, and all I did was lie there! My hip hurts, my foot is asleep, I limp for five minutes until I stop shaking, and now I'm stuck between Bubba and Blubba!

Then I remembered when I was in Baghdad. It was 140 degrees Fahrenheit, and on top of this, our soldiers, airmen, sailors, and marines are wearing eighty-five pounds of combat gear while living and working in harm's way with no opportunities to take a day off. They are running toward the sound of guns, willing to sacrifice their lives if necessary, so we can live with the peace of mind that we are safe and free.

How dare I complain about a sore back or go home from work because the air conditioner broke or take my freedom for granted! Suddenly, I stopped treating my fellow seatmates as objects and started talking to them as human beings. Everything was going to be fine. Then it happened.

The gentleman who was sitting next to me in first class came wandering to the back of the plane. When we made eye contact, I acknowledged him with a "What's up?"

He replied, "You made us all stop, think and feel guilty! When the next soldier got on the plane, I gave him my seat."

I smiled and replied, "Let me help you find yours."

Wouldn't you know it? He was seated in the row right in front of me in the center seat between two chubbier guys! He was so stuck he couldn't even turn around to keep complaining! Before we took off, four of us who had been sitting in first class were now sitting in the back of the plane to pay tribute to four soldiers who we should always honor, assist, and support.

But the story doesn't stop here. I checked into my hotel, had a great night's sleep, awoke refreshed and alert, put on my coat and tie, and entered the huge ballroom as the keynote speaker. Wouldn't you know it? The CEO who introduced me was the gentleman who was sitting next to me in first class. He read my standard introduction and then acknowledged to his 5,000 employees that I had inspired him and his colleagues to give up their seats to say thank you to our soldiers.

What is the moral to this story? People are watching. We are the message. It is not enough to just practice what we preach, we must preach only what we practice!

A Special Man

A FATHER CAME home from work and his little boy wanted him to play ball with him, but the father was too busy. The father explained, "I'd love to play, but I have too much work to do. But son, I want you to know that I love you." The little boy responded, "Daddy, I don't want you to love me. I want you to play ball with me." Put in his place, the guilty father masked his pain in a childish outburst, "Why don't you grow up?" His innocent boy shyly answered, "That's what I'm trying to do."

The father immediately softened to his son's profound reply. He picked him up in one arm and with the bat and ball in the other they headed to the park. One hour later his sweet little guy had taught him, "Any male can be a father, but it takes a special man to be a dad!"

Trust

A GROUP OF English botanists spent their vacation in the Swiss Alps collecting specimens and rare flowers. One morning they walked from a small village and came to a precipice. As they looked over a green valley, they located in their spotting scope a breathtaking field of peculiar flowers, which they knew was an incredible find if they could figure out how to retrieve at least one for their collection. From the cliff upon which they stood, to the valley floor, was a sheer drop of several hundred feet. To descend would be impossible, and to reach the valley from another approach would mean a delay of several hours.

During the latter part of their climb a small boy had joined the party and watched with interest as the botanists discussed the situation for several minutes. One of the men turned to the boy and said, "Young fellow, if you will let us tie a rope around your waist and lower you over a cliff so that you can dig up one of those plants for us, we'll pull you back up and give you $50."

The boy looked dazed for an instant, then ran off—apparently frightened at the prospect of being lowered over the cliff by a rope. But within a short time he returned, bringing with him a man, bent and gray, with hands gnarled and callused by hard labor. Upon reaching the party of botanists the boy turned to the man who had made the offer and said, "This is my dad. I'll go over the cliff if you'll let him hold the rope."

Promises

A YOUNG JAPANESE boy was spending the weekend with his elderly grandfather. The rendezvous would take place at the train station, for the grandfather lived in a village on the other side of the mountain. The boy's parents dropped him off, hugged both of them good-bye, and drove away.

As the two of them waited in line to buy their tickets, the grandfather discovered that he had left his wallet on the previous train. He didn't have any money and humbly asked the ticket lady if she would loan him yen valuing fifty dollars. The grandfather promised he would pay her back later that night.

Because of the Japanese culture's deep and abiding respect for its elders, the ticket lady believed the grandfather and paid for their tickets. An hour later, they arrived in the village. They walked fifteen minutes through the horrible weather and finally entered the cottage. Hungry, tired, and soaking wet, the grandfather went to his drawer and retrieved some money.

"Let's go," he said. His grandson rebutted, "But Grandfather, I'm starving and we're going back to the train station in three days. Why can't you just pay her back then? It will cost you the price of two more round-trip tickets to go now, just to pay back two one-way passes."

Putting on a dry overcoat and handing his grandson a wool blanket for comfort, the eighty-year-old grandfather put his arm around his grandson's shoulders and taught him the lesson of the ages. "Son, we must get there tonight before the counter closes and she goes home. This is not about money. This is about honor. I gave her my word, and we must always keep our promises!"

A Brother Like That

As a preacher, Dr. C. Roy Angell thought he understood the true meaning of friendship and love. Then it happened. His friend Paul received an automobile from his brother as a Christmas present. On Christmas Eve when Paul came out of his office, a street urchin was walking around the shiny new car, admiring it. "Is this your car, Mister?" he asked.

Paul nodded. "My brother gave it to me for Christmas." The boy was astounded.

"You mean your brother gave it to you and it didn't cost you nothing? Boy, I wish…" He hesitated. Of course Paul knew what he was going to wish for. He was going to wish he had a brother like that. But what the lad said jarred Paul all the way down to his heels.

"I wish," the boy went on, "that I could be a brother like that."

Paul looked at the boy in astonishment. Then he impulsively added, "Would you like to take a ride in my automobile?"

"Oh yes, I'd love that." After a short ride, the boy turned and with his eyes aglow said, "Mister, would you mind driving in front of my house?"

Paul smiled a little. He thought he knew what the lad wanted. He wanted to show his neighbors that he could ride home in a big automobile. But Paul was wrong again. "Will you stop where those two steps are?" the boy asked.

He ran up the steps. Then in a little while Paul heard him coming back, but he was not coming fast. He was carrying his little crippled brother. He sat him down on the bottom step, then sort of squeezed up against him and pointed to the car.

"There she is, Buddy, just like I told you upstairs. His brother gave it to him for Christmas and it didn't cost him a cent. And someday I'm gonna give you one just like it, then you can see for yourself all the pretty things in the Christmas windows that I've been trying to tell you about."

Paul got out and lifted the lad to the front seat of his car. The shining-eyed older brother climbed in beside him and the three of them began a memorable holiday ride. That Christmas Eve, Paul and Roy both learned what Jesus meant when he said, "It is more blessed to give…"

Trials

ONE DAY A man, who was not a believer in God, stopped at the little gorge to talk to his blacksmith friend, who had recently become a believer in God. Sympathizing with the blacksmith in some of his current trials, the man said, "It seems strange to me that so much affliction should come to you, just at the time when you have become a believer. I can't help wondering why it is."

The blacksmith answered, "You see the raw iron I have here to make into horseshoes. You know what I do with it? I take a piece and heat it in the fire until it is red, almost white with the heat. Then I hammer it unmercifully to shape it as I know it should be shaped. Then I plunge it into a pail of cold water to temper it.

Then I heat it again and hammer it some more. And this I do until it is finished. "But sometimes I find a piece of iron that won't stand up under this treatment. The heat and the hammering and the cold water are too much for it and it fails in the process." He pointed to a heap of scrap iron that was near the door of his shop.

"When I get a piece that cannot take the temperatures and hammering, I throw it out on the scrap heap. It will never be good for anything."

He finished his answer. "I know that God has been holding me in the fires of affliction, and I have felt life's hammer upon me. But I don't mind, if only He can bring me to what I should be. Try me in any way you wish, Lord, just don't throw me on the scrap heap!"

Forgive the Mistakes of Others

PAUL WAS NERVOUS as he sat on the train; the old man sitting next to him sensed this. "Son, what's the matter with you?"

"I just got out of prison," replied Paul. "My mistake broke my parents' hearts and caused them a lot of shame. I don't know if they can love me after what I did. I never let them visit me in prison. I told them they didn't have to let me come home if they were too ashamed of me. I live in a small town with a large tree by the railroad tracks. I told them to tie a ribbon around that old tree if they were willing to let me get off."

Paul paused as the old man listened, then continued. "The reason I'm so nervous is that we're almost there and I'm scared to look at that tree. I feel I don't deserve my parents' forgiveness because I hurt them so much."

Paul looked down in shame. Neither man spoke as the train slowed down to stop at the next station, Paul's hometown. Then the old man nudged him, "I think you can look now, son."

Paul glanced up slowly. The old tree was covered with ribbons—red, blue, yellow, orange, and green—hundreds of them. Paul turned to the old man with tears in his eyes and said, "They still love me. I'm going home."

Are You God?

ONE COLD EVENING during the holiday season, a little six year-old boy was standing out in front of a store window. The little child had no shoes and his clothes were mere rags. A young woman passing by saw the little boy and could read the longing in his pale blue eyes. She took the child by the hand and led him into the store. There she bought him some new shoes and a complete suit of warm clothing. They came back outside into the street and the woman said to the child, "Now you can go home and have a very happy holiday."

The little boy looked up at her and asked, "Are you God, Ma'am?" She smiled down at him and replied, "No son, I'm just one of His children."

The little boy smiled and excitedly slapped his leg, "I knew you had to be some relation!"

Leave No Regrets

IN A DEAR Abby newspaper column we are reminded to stop, look, listen, think, and feel before we act. (By Abigail Van Buren reprinted with permission of Universal Press Syndicate. All rights reserved.)

Dear Abby:

A young man from a wealthy family was about to graduate from high school. It was the custom in the affluent neighborhood for the parents to give the graduate an automobile. "Bill" and his father had spent months looking at various vehicles, and the week before graduation they found the perfect car. Bill was certain it would be his on graduation night.

Imagine his disappointment when, on the eve of his graduation, Bill's father handed him a gift-wrapped Bible! Bill was so angry he threw the Bible down and stormed out of the house. He and his father never saw each other again. It was the news of his father's death that brought Bill home again.

As he sat one night, going through his father's possessions that he was to inherit, he came across the Bible his father had given him. He brushed away the dust and opened it to find a cashier's check, dated the day of his graduation—in the exact amount of the car they had chosen together. Signed Beckah Fink, Texas

Dear Beckah;

I hope Bill read the Bible cover to cover, for it contained much he needed to learn: "A foolish son is a grief to his father, and bitterness to her who bore him." (Proverbs 17:25).

Plenty Of Time?

SATAN WAS MEETING with his top demons on how to tempt humanity to denounce Christianity and refuse to seek and find and follow Jesus. The first said, "We'll tell them there is no God."

The second demon said, "We'll let them believe there is a God, but we'll tell them Jesus isn't the Son of God."

The third demon said, "We'll tell them there is a God, and Jesus is the Son of God, but that the Bible is not the word of God."

Then the oldest, most experienced demon spoke up, "No. We'll tell them there is a God, that Jesus is the Son of God, and that the Bible is the word of God. What will destroy them fastest and forever is to tell them there is plenty of time."

Compassionate Service

A PROMINENT LOCAL businessman frequently brought his clients to a posh hotel to hold lunch meetings in the lobby restaurant. One day he showed up with his young son. When the boy excused himself to go to the washroom, the general manager asked the father what the special occasion was. The father sadly reported that his son had been diagnosed with cancer and that the next morning he would start his brutal chemotherapy treatments.

The father explained that he and his son were spending the night, and after their dinner, a dip in the pool, and a movie, the son was going to shave his head to prepare for the morning ordeal. Dad said his son knew he was going to lose his hair anyway and thought that by shaving it, he would be taking a more positive, proactive approach to fighting his cancer and controlling it instead of letting it control him. Dad explained that he too was going to shave his head in a sign of unconditional loving solidarity.

The father then asked the manager for a special favor, requesting that when they appeared the following morning for breakfast, the wait staff not react openly to their shaved heads or inquire about the reason they were both bald. Dad didn't want them to embarrass his son at what was to be the start of the most challenging period of his life.

When dad and son arrived for breakfast, nobody in the room batted an eyelid or said a word. Two of the waiters, however, had also shaved their heads that night too.

Perspective

IF TWO PEOPLE are looking out the same window at the same lashing rainstorm and one complains: 'What a horrible day' – and the other one exclaims: 'What a wonderful day' – the weather did not change! When we change the way we look at things, the things we look at change.

For example, a famous shoe manufacturer in England sent two sales representatives to Africa to see if there might be an opportunity to open up a new market and sell more shoes. Both reps returned to London and reported. The first sales professional said, "Nobody in Africa wears shoes. So, there is no market for our products there." The second sales professional reported, "Nobody in Africa wears shoes. So, there's a huge opportunity to open up a new market and sell thousands of shoes in Africa!"

Who Are You - Really?

YOLANDA WAS HIRED at a corporation as the administrative assistant to the CEO. At the beginning of the company national convention, Yolanda was invited on stage to sing the National Anthem. No one in the company knew she could sing and before she had even finished the song, the crowd began to cheer and continued to cheer and stomp and whistle and clap for at least two minutes afterward. Truly she had blown everyone's mind, and people commented, "As good as Whitney Houston and Jennifer Hudson" and "the next Beyoncé."

Question: Is Yolanda an administrative assistant who happens to be a phenomenal superstar singer - or is Yolanda a superstar singer who happens to be an administrative assistant?

The answer to this question is the beginning of identifying who you really are. Yes, it is important for us to never live 'small' and to always work hard to accomplish great things. But when we identify ourselves in terms of what we do instead of who we are, we become human doings instead of human beings – unacceptable if significance is what we seek.

Who we really are is about what we really believe, so we are always the same off stage as we are on stage – especially when times get so tough that we feel we've hit 'rock bottom.' You see, no one ever hits 'rock bottom' – we hit rock foundation – we hit rock belief – we hit the core values and fundamental truths on which we were raised. Whenever our organizations go through a tough time – they don't hit rock bottom – they hit the baseline governing principles on which they were built.

Are your beliefs strong enough, deep enough and true enough to equip you to proactively respond to rapid change – right now? It's like ordering an 'UBER' ride that requires you enter in your current location. If you lie about where you are, the directions won't work! Becoming a superstar begins with what you believe and who you really are - right now!

Experienced Hammer

A YOUNG COLLEGE student called a plumber to his home to solve a serious problem. Soon an elderly gentleman arrived, but before he was invited in, the young man questioned why he didn't have a toolbox. The plumber smiled and quietly replied, 'Tell me what the problem is.' The young man explained that every time he flushed his toilet or turned on the water in the sink the pipes make a loud, horrific thumping noise that shakes the house.

The plumber looked around and listened for about 10 minutes, grabbed a small hammer from his pocket, walked straight to a section of the pipe and hit it twice in the same spot. 'That should do it,' he said.

Sure enough, when the young man turned on the water and flushed the toilet, the problem had been fixed. The plumber smiled, left the bill on the table, and departed. Moments later the young man looked at the bill and immediately phoned the plumber to complain, 'Why did you charge me $201 dollars? You were only here for fifteen minutes max and only used a tiny hammer!'

The plumber quietly answered, 'The bill is itemized at the bottom of the page: $2 dollars for hitting the pipe twice. $199 dollars for knowing why, where and how to hit it!'

Wanted: A Real Mother

MARY KING SAT before the dressing table in her bedroom holding in her hands a worn copy of a book, The Velveteen Rabbit and a string of beads—pearls they were, old, tarnished. As Mary looked at them her eyes blazed with anger. Tomorrow was her graduation day from high school. All day she had been at the class picnic and she had had such a glorious time. They had danced and played, they had rowed on the lake and sung their school songs in the moonlight. She had been happy as a girl could be, and to have it spoiled in this way was cruel. Why should her mother give her a book and a string of old beads for a graduation present?

Other girls had wrist watches, pretty dresses, checks, and all sorts of beautiful things. When they asked her what her mother's gift had been, how could she say, "A book and old beads?" Mother would expect her to wear them at their graduation; how could she? She had found them on her table when she came into her room. With them was a note saying:

Dear Mary,

I waited for you to come home so that I could give you my gift, but it is so late and I am too tired to wait any longer, so I will leave it for you. I could not buy you a real gift, so I have given you the dearest things I have. The book has a special message and every bead has a story which some day I will tell you—perhaps on the day you graduate from college, but not now. I hope you will love them as I do. I shall see them tomorrow on your pretty new dress. Good night, Mary, I hope you had a good time.

Love,
Mother

Why was mother so queer? All her life it had been hard for Mary to have her mother so different. Her mother worked for Mr. Morse and so she could never bring her friends to their rooms, lest she should annoy the Morse's. Other girls' mothers had pretty faces, and her mother's face was all red and cross-looking. Other girls' mothers had pretty hair, but her mother had straight hair and little of it. She had tried to get her to wear false hair, but instead of doing it, her mother had gone to her room and cried because Mary had suggested it.

Other girls' mothers let them wear pretty clothes, but hers were always plain, though they were always very neat. Most of the girls had fancy new graduation dresses, but hers was only a little dimity that her mother had made—and now this book and these dreadful beads were more than she could stand and she threw them on the bed in anger. She wished she had "real gifts" and a "real mother" of whom she could be "really" proud.

As she started to take down her long wavy hair, she saw a letter in Mr. Morse's handwriting on her desk. Perhaps this was a check for her graduation present, so she hastily tore it open. But no check dropped out. Instead, there was a long letter, and she sat down to read.

"My dear Mary," it began. "A few days ago, I chanced to be on the beach when you were there with your friend, and I heard you say to her, 'I wish my mother were as beautiful as yours. Mother can't even go down the street with me for she drags her foot so that everybody turns and looks at us, and it makes me feel so conspicuous. You must be very proud of your mother.' So I have decided that for your graduation, I shall give you a story instead of the check that I had intended to give you."

"A story," said Mary to herself. "That is worse than the old book and beads. What a house of queer people this is! Anyway, I am curious to see what sort of story he could write."

So she read on. "Seventeen years ago there came to town in the eastern part of Pennsylvania a young man and his bride. Just a slip of a girl she was, but her face was full of sunshine, and everyone soon loved her. She had beautiful, wavy hair and bright, blue eyes and a cherry smile. After they had been there for a while, their story came to be known, for his father was a great mill owner in a nearby town. When the young man had married the high school girl out of real love instead of the wealthy girl whom the father had chosen for him, there had been a lot of trouble and the young man had been told to leave home with his bride and expect no more help from the father.

"Now the young man had never worked, so it was very hard for him. She was now pregnant, but she also worked and, little by little, they bought the things needed in the tiny home on the hill, and they were very happy. Then, one day a scaffold fell and they brought the young husband to the little wife all bruised and bleeding. And that very night a tiny girl was born into the world who came to the home to live. The neighbors helped all they could, but in a few days the father of the baby died and the little young wife was left alone to care for the baby.

"When the mill-owner heard of the death of the son and the birth of the little girl, he sent to the mother and said, 'We will take the little girl and bring her up as our own if you will give her to us and have no more to do with her.' But the brave little woman sent back her answer, 'As long as I have a mind with which to think and two hands with which to work, I can and will support my little girl.'

"But it was a hard pull. She worked in an office; she worked on a farm. Then a position was offered her as a teacher in a home for children. Here she could have her own room and keep the baby with her. When she was not teaching, it would be cared for with the others. Gladly, the mother took the position and for more than a year she was very, very happy.

"One night when the baby was nearly three years old, she sat reading in the parlor of the home when someone called, 'Fire, fire! Fire in the left wing!' Oh! That was where her baby was, on the very top floor. Like a bird she flew across the hall where the smoke already was pouring out. Up the first flight, choking, she went. Up to the second. Then she had to fall to the floor to creep along. She could see the fire. It was on the fourth floor where Mary was. Could she ever reach it? Would the fire block her way?

"Ten minutes after the call of fire had been given, the workers saw someone staggering through the lower hall. In her arms she carried a bundle wrapped tightly in a quilt. Dangling from one hand was a long string of beads and from the other a small book called The Velveteen Rabbit. Her face was burned. There was no hair on her head. She was writhing in agony, but she reached the door, handed the bundled baby to the worker, saying quietly, 'I am badly burned, but I have saved my three treasures. Keep them safe for me!' Then she fell in a heap on the floor.

"For months and months she tossed on a bed of pain. No one thought she could possibly live. But she did, for she was living for her baby. When at last she came from the hospital, her beautiful face was scarred and red; only in spots had the hair grown back; her hands were stiff and painful; and one leg dragged as she walked. But she was alive, and that was all she asked.

"While she had been ill, I had gone to see the mill-owner to ask for help for the brave little woman who had shown us all what a heroine she was. But his answer had been, 'She took my son from me and I will have nothing to do with her. If she will give the child to me, I will bring it up in luxury, but I will not have her here.'

"So when she was ready to go back to work, I told her that another offer had come from the grandfather of the child to adopt it and I said to her, 'Don't you feel that you had better give him the baby?'

"She humbly answered, 'If I can fight death for my baby, I can conquer in the fight to live. I shall keep her. You may tell him that the child will not live in luxury but that she shall know no want, and she shall have both the education and the culture which befits her father's child.'

"As one can imagine, the mother's heart was sore each time she looked in the mirror and saw what a pitiful change had come to her pretty face. 'I am glad it came while Mary was little,' she said. 'Had it come later, she would have minded my ugly face. Now she knows no better and she will grow used to it.'

"So she was glad when I offered to have her come to live with us in the distant city where none had known of her or of the awful fight she was planning to make. We had taken a large house and there were many things the mother could do with her stiff hands which gradually, because of the long hours she had spent on them, were beginning to limber up a bit. I gave her rooms for herself and the child, and there she lived, keeping away from all so that none might see her shrunken, changed body. She lived only for the child, hoarding carefully the little money she could save lest there be not enough to send her to college when high school should be over.

"Often have I heard her praying for strength to fight through the battle; often have I begged her to let me tell the child the story of the days that had gone, but her answer was always the same, 'No. Let her live the happy, carefree life. Someday I will tell her, but not now. It would kill me to have her pity me. She must love me for myself and not for what I did. My only happiness is to live and work for her.'

"To my way of thinking, she is a real hero, a mother of whom you may be proud. She must never know I have told you. For it would add to her burden if she thought for a minute she was not all that you wanted your mother to be. "Sincerely, "A.E. Morse"

When Mary had finished the letter, she sat stunned. Frantically she picked up the pearls she had thrown on the bed. Her mother had carried them with her through that awful fire! They were one of her three treasures, and she had almost said she would not wear them. Oh, what a selfish girl she had been! She had thought only of herself. And the book? She must have carried it through the fire as well. Once Mary had asked her mother why the scar was on her face and why the limp and misshapen hands and knot of hair, and she had answered, 'Just an accident, child, when I was a young woman." Then she had talked of something else. Every minute since she was born, she had been a burden to her mother.

Overcome with emotion, she cried as she remembered that it had been years since Mother had had a new dress, but she had thought it was because she was weird. There had been many days when mother had seemed cross. Was it because she was suffering? Oh, how sorry she was! What could she do to make her happy, now that she knew?

Slowly Mary prepared for bed. She must be in the dark to think. When she knelt in prayer, she asked God to forgive her—but she remembered that she could not ask her mother to do so. She remembered the words of her mother to Mr. Morse: "It would kill me to have her feel sorry for me. She must love me for myself and not for what I did."

Mary tossed and tumbled as the time slipped by. Suddenly she heard a foot dragging across the hall, and a big lump came into her throat. How often she had rebelled at that foot! Then her mother came quietly into the room.

"Mother," said Mary, "Why are you here? Aren't you asleep yet?"

"No, dear," she said, and the girl thought she had never heard a more beautiful voice. "I heard you tossing in bed and I thought perhaps you were ill so I came to see. What is the trouble, dear?"

"Oh, tomorrow is my graduation day and I think I am sorry to leave school," said Mary. "I love these dear little beads which I have under the pillow, Mother. And I'm so excited to read the book. Have you had them long? I never saw them before."

"Many, many years, Mary. Your father gave them to me and how hard he worked to earn them. I love every little bead on the string. I shall love to see you wear them for his sake. I saved them for you once long ago because I wanted you to have something that he had earned for us. And the little book is the book your father gave me on our wedding night. He said the message epitomized our relationship and love. And now you just go to sleep, for you must look bright and pretty tomorrow. Oh! I shall be so proud of you when you receive your diploma!"

Mary gently reached up and drew her mother down close to the bed, and whispered, "Be all ready when the carriage comes for me tomorrow, Mother dear, for you are going with me. It's been a long time since I've told you, but I love you with all of my heart. I'm proud of you and tomorrow I can't wait to introduce you to all of my friends."

As Mary's mother left her bedroom, Mary clicked on her light and began to read. From the pages of her gift book, the Velveteen Rabbit asked, "What is real?" Mary smiled and fell fast asleep now knowing the special message.

Parable of the Eagle

A FARMER IN Wyoming was walking through the forest and found a newborn eagle that had fallen from its nest. He took it home, nursed it back to full strength, and put it in the chicken coop to raise it. A few years later, a Native American naturalist stopped by the farmer's house and noticed the full-grown bird. "What is that eagle doing in the chicken coop? It isn't right that an eagle should be kept with chickens."

The Native American picked up the bird and said, "Thou hast the heart of an eagle. Thou dost belong to the sky and not to the earth. Stretch forth thy wings and fly."

The bird looked around outside its comfort zone, but quickly saw the chickens and dropped to the ground. "See, I told you it was a chicken," the farmer bragged. "I have raised it as a chicken, and it thinks and pecks and walks like a chicken."

The naturalist exclaimed, "No, no, it is a mighty eagle." He took the bird and stood on top of the farmer's shed. "Stretch forth thy wings and fly," he said. But once again, the eagle saw its chicken friends below and jumped down to peck with them.

Early the next morning, the naturalist revisited the farm and took the bird from the chicken coop to the base of a great mountain. In classic Native American tradition, he held the bird high over his head and bellowed loud enough for his voice to echo and bounce off the cliff walls. "Thou art an eagle. Thou hast the heart of an eagle. Thou dost belong to the wind and the sky and not unto the earth. Stretch forth thy wings and fly."

The eagle looked down uncomfortably, but the naturalist forced it to look directly into the sun. A moment passed and then, with a screech, it stretched forth its wings and flew.

Sometimes we fail to dream mighty dreams and fail to soar to the heights that the eagle in each of us can attain because we have our eyes down with the chickens. We are pecking and grabbing about because we lack self-confidence and self-esteem. And so we minimize our own worth. We are groping because we're missing the link that connects us from where we are to where we want to be. Don't you think it is now time to start seeing yourself as you really are, an eagle soaring above the average, negative crowd? You were born to succeed. Stretch forth your wings and fly!

Clark's Credo

I'm smart, talented, and I never say never.

I'm wanted, important, lovable,
capable, and I can succeed.

I'm a good athlete, I love music,
and I get good grades in school.

I never say "I can't"—I always say "I can, I will."

If I fall down, I just get back up and go again.

If I spill or make a mistake, I learn why,
clean it up, and say "no big deal."

I love God and will do the right thing
simply because it's the right thing to do!

I always treat others as I want to be treated and leave
my family, friends, job, neighborhood, country, and
world in better shape than I found them, so when we
are apart they say: "I like me best when I'm with you. I
want to see you again."

Printed in the USA
CPSIA information can be obtained
at www.ICGtesting.com
LVHW011327221123
764524LV00082BA/3572

9 781088 234914